I0347544

MINDFUL POETIC REFLECTIONS DURING & AFTER CANCER

365 DAILY REFLECTIONS & AFFIRMATIONS

CAROLINE DAVID-TOSTEVIN

Poetic Trend
PUBLISHING

Mindful Poetic Reflections During & After Cancer: 365 Daily Reflections & Affirmations
Copyright © 2025 Caroline David-Tostevin

First Published 2025 by Poetic Trend Publishing.

ISBN - Paperback : 978-1-9192285-1-8
ISBN - Hardcover : 978-1-9192285-2-5
ISBN - eBook (Print Replica) : 978-1-9192285-0-1
ISBN - eBook (Reflowable) : 978-1-9192285-3-2

Book cover design adapted from image templates by @raizencreativestudio and @elenkoss.

The right of Caroline David-Tostevin to be identified as the author of this work has been asserted in accordance with the Copyright, Design and Patents Act, 1988.

All rights reserved. No part of this book may be reproduced, distributed, or transmitted in any form or by any means, including photocopying, recording, or other electronic or mechanical methods, without the prior written permission of the publisher, except in the case of brief quotations embodied in critical reviews and certain other non-commercial uses permitted by copyright law. For permission requests, write to the publisher.

We apologise for any inaccuracies that may have occurred and will resolve inaccurate or missing information in a subsequent reprinting of the book.

This publication is sold under the express understanding that any decisions or actions you take as a result of reading this book must be based on your own judgement and will be at your sole risk. The author will not be held responsible for the consequences of any actions and/or decisions taken as a result of any information given or recommendations made.

A CiP catalogue record for this book is available from the British Library.

Introduction

A Journey Through Words and Healing

In the quiet folds of 2024, when the shadow of a breast cancer diagnosis fell across my path, I found myself seeking solace in the gentle rhythms of mindfulness and the tender embrace of self-care. This journey, though daunting, was illuminated by the compassionate hands of my treatment team, the nurturing guidance of Penny Brohn UK, and the steadfast support of MacMillan Cancer Support. Their care became a beacon, guiding me through the tempests of treatment and into the calm waters of recovery. Yet, it was through the transformative experiences of Breast Cancer Now's 'Moving Forward' programme and Life After Cancer's 'Creativity for Wellbeing' course that I rediscovered a spark within—a fervent desire to weave my emotion into words, to transform pain into poetry, and to craft a legacy of resilience through the art of writing.

From my earliest days, words and music have been my sanctuary, a place where my heart could unfold without fear. As a child, I would ose myself in the cadence of a poem or the melody of a song, finding refuge in their ability to hold both joy and sorrow. During the long months of treatment, when uncertainty loomed like a winter storm, journaling became my haven. Each word scratched onto the page was a step toward understanding, a way to cradle my fears and hopes alike. What began as private reflections soon blossomed into poetry, songwriting, and creative works—each piece a delicate thread in the tapestry of my emotional voyage. Some of these writings were later brought to life in album songs, *Still Here*, where evocative melodies intertwine with verses that honour both my journey and the unwavering love of those who walked beside me. Available on all major streaming platforms, this collection is a testament to the enduring power of creativity to heal and uplift.

I draw boundless inspiration from the tranquil beauty of nature—the whisper of wind through ancient oaks, the soft ripple of a stream under February's frost, or the fleeting dance of a sparrow across a snowy field. The delights of travel, with its allure of uncharted horizons, and the profound warmth of family and motherhood, deeply inspire my creative works. In the quiet moments of my own journey with cancer, this book took shape as a collection of mindful poetic reflections, written to walk alongside those facing cancer therapies, recovery, and the brighter days that follow. During the challenges of treatment and the tender steps toward healing, writing and reading these poetic reflections became my haven, urging me to pause and notice the gentle beauty around me. The whisper of leaves in the wind, the loyal gaze of a pet, the soft warmth of sunlight on my face—these simple wonders grounded me, reminding me to cherish every breath, every person, and every fleeting moment. They wove a sense of gratitude and strength into my days, turning hardship into a deeper appreciation for life's gifts.

These poetic reflections were penned not only for my own solace but for the countless others who may tread similar paths, perhaps yet to discover the balm of mindful contemplation. Each verse remains a radiant touchstone, infusing my days with purpose and casting a soft glow upon the path ahead with hope's gentle light. I offer them as a tender summons to others—to behold the subtle wonders of nature, to feel the heartbeat of human connection, and to savour the exquisite beauty of simply being alive. In sharing these words, I extend a hand across the silence, yearning to kindle in others the same enduring light that has guided me through the shadows and into the tender embrace of each dawning day.

This book is more than a collection of words; it is an offering, a small light cast into the darkness for anyone who finds themselves walking a path that feels insurmountable. To those standing at the edge of their own impossible, I hope these pages—woven from my heart's quiet triumphs and tender reflections—might offer solace, courage, or even a moment of recognition. May they remind you that even in the coldest winter, there is warmth to be found, and in the stillest moments, a gentle rhythm persists, carrying you forward with grace and hope.

TABLE of CONTENTS

JANUARY	1
FEBRUARY	19
MARCH	37
APRIL	55
MAY	73
JUNE	91
JULY	105
AUGUST	121
SEPTEMBER	139
OCTOBER	155
NOVEMBER	171
DECEMBER	187

JANUARY

1st January – Monthly Opening Poem

New Light

A new year rises with soft, gentle light,
Pale morning glows, tender and bright.
Yesterday's shadows lie still and deep,
Today unfolds with promises to keep.
Breath by breath, step by step, you move,
Carrying hope, courage, and quiet love.
Each budding leaf, each whispering breeze,
Speaks of renewal and moments of ease.
Nature's hush settles soft and wide,
A calm companion, a faithful guide.
January beckons, patient and true,
"I hold gentle courage here for you."
In every step, in every glance,
You meet the year with quiet stance.
Embrace the stillness, let it grow,
And feel the warmth of life's soft flow.

Affirmation: You begin this year with hope, calm, and gentle strength.

2nd January
The Stillness of Snow

Snow blankets the world in soft, white quiet, transforming the familiar into whispers of serenity. You mirror this stillness within yourself, noticing the peace that emerges when you pause. Even in moments of fatigue or worry, your spirit can rest and renew. Today, move slowly and intentionally, letting thoughts and muscles soften. Each quiet moment, each gentle pause, is a reminder of the resilience that dwells within you. Let stillness guide your heart, restoring calm and fortitude with every breath.

Affirmation: Stillness nurtures and strengthens you from within.

3rd January
Frosted Mornings

As January's frosty veil drapes the countryside, the dawn reveals a world where every twig and blade is adorned with nature's delicate filigree, glinting like stars fallen to earth. The blackbird's song, piercing the cold silence, carries a melody of endurance, a reminder that beauty thrives even in winter's austere embrace. Observe the squirrel, nimble and determined, foraging beneath the skeletal boughs of the ash, its quiet industry a testament to life's persistent pulse. In this season of sparseness, where the earth slumbers beneath a quilt of frost, your own resilience mirrors the steadfast yew, rooted deep in the frozen ground yet ever green. Each step you take through this crystalline morning is a quiet act of defiance against the cold, a spark of warmth kindled within. Let the gentle mist that curls through the valleys guide your thoughts to peace, for in the heart of winter, your spirit shines with the soft, unyielding glow of a distant sun. Embrace this moment, for every breath is a silent hymn to your enduring strength.

Affirmation: You find resilience and grace in subtle, gentle ways.

4th January
The Whisper of Renewal

Winter air carries a hush of possibility, soft but insistent, calling to your heart. You notice the small stirrings of hope within yourself, encouraging gentle progress and quiet trust. Today, each breath, each pause, each mindful step is a part of your renewal. Even when uncertainty tugs, your spirit remains steady, guided by inner calm. Let this quiet energy ripple through your day, reminding you that healing, growth, and strength unfold in their own time.

Affirmation: Stillness nurtures and strengthens you from within.

5th January
Silver Light

In the tender embrace of a January morning, where silver light spills from a veiled winter sky, the world is bathed in a quiet radiance that softens the starkness of frost-kissed meadows. The delicate trill of a wren, flitting through the bare branches of a hawthorn, weaves a thread of hope through the chill air, its small form a beacon of life's persistence. As you stand beneath the vast, pale canopy, let the enduring grace of the willow, bending yet unbroken by the winter's weight, mirror the quiet strength within your soul. Each breath you draw is a silent echo of the deer, stepping softly through the mist, its eyes gleaming with unspoken resolve. In this season of stillness, where the earth cradles its dreams beneath a blanket of frost, your every gesture is a testament to resilience, like the faint tracks of a badger etched in the snow. Let the gentle glow of this silver light guide your heart, illuminating the smallest victories, for even in the heart of winter, your spirit dances with the promise of spring's renewal.

Affirmation: You carry light and strength within yourself at every moment.

6th January
The Gift of Slowness

Moving slowly today allows you to notice the beauty of small details, the soft rhythms of your own breath, and the gentle pulse of life around you. There is courage in careful steps, and wisdom in measured pauses. Today, let each moment unfold with intention, giving space for reflection, calm, and renewal. Even in the quietest acts, your spirit grows stronger, more aware, more patient. Slowness is not weakness; it is a tender, sustaining power that nourishes your heart and soul.

Affirmation: You embrace the strength found in gentle, mindful movement.

7th January
Winter's Whisper

The frost lies quiet upon the ground,
A gentle hush, a peaceful sound.
Branches bow beneath the pale white sky,
Yet reach upward, steady and high.
Even in cold, the world persists,
Each whisper of wind a quiet gift.
Your spirit moves with similar grace,
Finding courage in this still space.
Step softly through the winter light,
Let calm and patience guide your night.
Hope glimmers in each gentle breath,
A quiet promise beyond the frost's depth.
Every small pause, each mindful glance,
Carries resilience, invites you to dance.
Through days of stillness, shadows, and white,
You hold a steady, enduring light.
Trust in its rhythm, slow and true,
Winter carries renewal for you.

Affirmation: You move through challenges with gentle grace and enduring hope.

8th January
The Flow of Quiet Days

Winter days stretch with soft, muted light, inviting reflection and calm. You notice the subtle rhythms of your body, the slow rise and fall of breath, and the quiet steadiness of your mind. Today, move through each moment intentionally, with gentle awareness. Every act — a mindful pause, a quiet thought, a soft step — strengthens your resilience and honours your journey. Even when the world feels cold or heavy, your spirit carries warmth and calm. Allow yourself to breathe deeply and flow slowly through your day.

Affirmation: You embrace each day with calm, patience, and quiet resilience.

9th January
Snowed-In Moments

In the heart of January's embrace, where snow blankets the earth in a hush of white, the world pauses, yet beneath this frozen veil, life stirs with quiet tenacity, like the dormouse nestled in its hidden burrow, dreaming through the cold. The soft tread of a fox across the snow-draped heath leaves fleeting imprints, a reminder that even in stillness, movement persists in the subtlest forms. As you linger in these snowed-in moments, let the ancient yew, cloaked in frost yet evergreen, reflect the enduring strength that resides within you. Each breath you take is a delicate thread, weaving hope through the winter's silence, much like the sparrow's gentle chirp that pierces the icy air. In this season of repose, where the landscape slumbers under a quilt of snow, your pauses are acts of grace, nurturing your spirit as the earth nurtures the seeds beneath its frozen surface. Let the soft glow of a winter moon guide your thoughts to peace, for in the stillness of these moments, your soul shines with a quiet, radiant courage, blooming softly amidst the frost.

Affirmation: You carry hidden strength and quiet hope within you.

10th January
Crystal Branches

Branches glint with frost, delicate yet resilient, mirroring the quiet endurance within you. Each mindful breath and measured step affirms your inner strength. Today, notice this resilience and let it warm your heart. Even in moments of fatigue or uncertainty, your spirit holds steady. Each gentle action, each pause, each thought is an affirmation of courage. Trust in your luminous, enduring strength, and allow it to guide your steps through every winter day.

Affirmation: You are resilient and luminous in all seasons.

11th January
The Subtle Light of Hope

Even in the quietest winter, light exists — subtle, persistent, guiding. You feel it rising softly within your chest, a gentle companion through each challenge. Today, allow hope to illuminate your path, inspiring courage and patience. Each breath, each pause, each small act of care becomes a spark of renewal. Trust the light that always remains, even when shadows linger. Let it steady you, fill you, and carry you with calm assurance.

Affirmation: Hope rises softly within you, guiding and sustaining your spirit.

12th January
The Grace of Slowness

Slow, deliberate movements bring awareness and calm. Today, notice the gentle rhythm of your breath and the tender pulse of your heart. Even small gestures, slow steps, and quiet thoughts carry strength and intention. Let this grace fill your day, nourishing both body and spirit. Each mindful act is a testament to your resilience and patience. Moving slowly is a soft power, a sustaining force, and a profound act of self-care.

Affirmation: You move with grace, patience, and quiet strength.

13th January
Winter's Heart

In the deep embrace of January's chill, where the air shimmers with the crystalline breath of winter, the landscape holds a quiet majesty, like the steadfast oak standing sentinel over frost-dusted fields. The red deer, with its velvet antlers cutting through the mist, moves with a grace that echoes the silent strength within your own heart. Far from the shore, the grey seal basks on icy rocks, its sleek form a testament to resilience amidst the sea's wintry tumult. As you tread through this pale, frosted world, let the glowing embers of a distant hearth mirror the warmth that burns steadily within you. Each breath you draw is a pulse of life, akin to the gentle ripple of a winter stream, carving its path beneath a veneer of ice. In this season of quietude, where the earth cradles its secrets beneath a mantle of snow, your every gesture is a spark of light, like the fleeting glimpse of a kingfisher darting over a frozen river. Trust in the rhythm of your inner flame, for it guides you through the winter's heart with luminous courage, a beacon glowing softly against the cold.

Affirmation: You carry warmth and resilience within your heart.

14th January
The Winter Light

The world is still beneath pale skies,
A quiet hush where beauty lies.
Frosted branches glint with grace,
A gentle glow on winter's face.
Even when shadows linger near,
Light whispers softly, calm and clear.
Each breath you take is a gentle flame,
A quiet strength you cannot name.
Step lightly through each frozen street,
Feel courage rising with each heartbeat.
Patience wraps you in its gentle fold,
Stories of quiet triumph told.
Through every trial, each snowy night,
You carry warmth and steady light.
Trust in this rhythm, slow and bright,
Winter holds renewal for you tonight.

Affirmation: You are guided by gentle light, calm, and enduring strength.

15th January
Snow and Stillness

The world sleeps beneath snow, and you mirror its quiet, soft rhythm. Each breath is deliberate, each pause a gentle act of care for yourself. Even in moments of fatigue or worry, your spirit remains luminous, steady, and enduring. Today, notice how stillness can be a source of strength, a place where resilience quietly blooms. Let your heart soften, your thoughts settle, and your mind rest. Each small movement, each mindful pause, carries calm and courage, nurturing your inner light.

Affirmation: Stillness nurtures your spirit and strengthens your courage.

16th January
Frost-Kissed Awareness

Frost glimmers on windowpanes, delicate yet persistent, a mirror of your own quiet endurance. Today, notice the subtle details around you — the shimmer of ice, the hush of air, the gentle warmth in your chest. Each observation grounds you, reminding you that life continues even in stillness. Let your awareness carry you softly through the day, giving care to your body, mind, and heart. Even small breaths and quiet moments are triumphs of patience, hope, and resilience.

Affirmation: You notice and honour the subtle beauty in every moment.

17th January
The Gentle Pace

Move today with deliberate gentleness, like the soft flow of winter light across snowed-in fields. There is no rush, no demand, only the steady rhythm of your own presence. Each breath anchors you, each pause restores you, and each step, however small, builds quiet resilience. In embracing this gentle pace, you honour the enduring strength within yourself. Let your heart expand with calm, your spirit rest in trust, and your body feel supported in every movement.

Affirmation: You move through life with calm, steady purpose and quiet strength.

18th January
The Subtle Strength of Winter

In the quiet chill of a January morning, where frost blankets the fields in a delicate shimmer, nature holds a gentle strength, like the sturdy oak standing firm against the winter breeze. The hare, bounding softly through the snow-dusted grass, carries a quiet resolve, its swift movements a sign of life's persistence. By the coast, the seal glides through icy waters, its steady grace a reminder of endurance in the cold. As you walk through this frosty world, let the calm of a frozen stream, still flowing beneath its icy surface, reflect the strength within your heart. Each breath you take is like the patient fox, waiting in the shadows for the right moment to move. In this season of winter's calm, where the earth rests under a layer of snow, your every step and quiet thought is a small triumph. Trust this inner spark, for like the faint glow of moonlight on the snow, it shines with a steady, gentle truth.

Affirmation: You carry quiet strength and resilience in every moment.

19th January
The Warmth Within

Though frost blankets the earth outside, warmth resides in your heart. Today, let this inner fire guide you — warming your thoughts, nurturing your spirit, and sustaining your courage. Even when days feel long or challenging, your heart carries a gentle, unwavering light. Notice it in every act of kindness toward yourself, every pause for reflection, and every breath that grounds you. You are your own safe haven, a source of calm and reassurance.

Affirmation: You nurture warmth and light within yourself every day.

20th January
The Winter River

A river flows beneath the ice,
Hidden, quiet, calm, precise.
Though snow may cover its gentle stream,
Its waters continue, a silent dream.
So too does your spirit quietly move,
Through trials, stillness, and acts of love.
Each breath you take is a tiny wave,
Each pause a current, steady and brave.
Even in shadow, the river shines,
Carrying hope through frozen pines.
Step softly along its winding course,
Let patience guide, a gentle force.
The world may slow, the winds may bite,
Yet the river flows with quiet light.
Trust its rhythm, deep and true,
It carries renewal and strength to you.

Affirmation: You move with life's currents, carrying hope and quiet courage.

21st January
Crystal Moments

In the gentle hush of a January dawn, where frost traces delicate patterns on the hedgerows, nature offers fleeting glimpses of beauty, like the slender birch adorned with icy jewels. The robin, with its bright chest aglow against the snow, hops lightly across the frozen ground, a small emblem of life's quiet endurance. Along the winter shore, the puffin bobs on the chilly waves, its steadfast presence a spark of resilience amid the sea's cold embrace. As you pause in this frosted world, let the soft glimmer of sunlight through a misty cloud mirror the steady strength within your soul. Each breath you take is a moment of calm, like the dormouse curled snugly in its winter nest, safe in the stillness. In this season of crisp air and quiet earth, your gentle attention to these crystal moments weaves a tapestry of gratitude. Linger in their glow, for like the faint twinkle of stars on a snowy night, they reflect the enduring light of your heart.

Affirmation: You notice and cherish the enduring beauty in every moment.

22nd January
The Patience of Snow

Snow does not hurry, yet it transforms the world with quiet persistence. Today, let patience guide your steps and thoughts. Each pause, each mindful action, is part of the gentle unfolding of your strength. You do not need to rush; your presence is enough. Even slow progress nurtures the heart, builds resilience, and restores calm. Trust the rhythm of your own unfolding, for it is steady, true, and entirely sufficient.

Affirmation: Patience nurtures and strengthens you in all that you do.

23rd January
Light Through Frost

Even in the quietest, frost-covered days, light pierces through, subtle and soft. Today, let this gentle illumination fill your mind and heart. Notice the way hope rises quietly, like sunlight reflecting on icy branches. Each mindful thought, each soft breath, is a spark of light guiding you forward. Even when days feel heavy or uncertain, the light within you remains present, steady, and unwavering.

Affirmation: Light and hope shine within you, steady and true.

24th January
The Strength of Reflection

Winter invites reflection, a gentle pause to consider where you have been and where you are heading. Today, honour your journey — every challenge faced, every moment of courage, every breath of patience. Let reflection deepen your awareness, nurture your resilience, and fill you with gentle gratitude. Each quiet thought, each mindful pause, is a testament to the strength that endures, even in stillness.

Affirmation: Reflection strengthens your heart, mind, and spirit.

25th January
The Lanterns of Winter

Lanterns glow along the snowy streets,
Soft circles of warmth where shadow meets.
Even in cold, their light persists,
A gentle guide through quiet mists.
Your heart is a lantern, steady and true,
Illuminating paths in softest hue.
Through long nights and days of frost,
It shines for the joys that are not lost.
Each breath a flame, each thought a spark,
A quiet fire to light the dark.
Let hope and patience be your guide,
With courage walking at your side.
Even when winds of winter blow,
Your inner light continues to grow.
Trust its warmth, soft yet bright,
It carries you through every night.

Affirmation: Your inner light guides you with warmth, hope, and courage.

26th January
The Calm of Snow

In the tender stillness of a January day, where snow falls gently to cloak the hills in a soft white hush, nature weaves a quiet haven, like the ancient pine standing serene under its snowy mantle. The red squirrel, scampering lightly across the frosted branches, carries a spark of life that warms the winter's silence. By the rugged coast, the gannet dives through the icy spray, its steadfast grace a reminder of resilience amid the sea's chill. As you tread softly through this tranquil world, let the calm of a snow-draped meadow reflect the steady peace within your heart. Each deep breath you draw mirrors the patient badger, resting in its sett, enduring the cold with quiet strength. In this season of muffled sounds and gentle snow, your smallest actions ripple like the soft tracks of a deer across a frozen field. Embrace this winter's hush, for like the faint glow of a lantern on a snowy night, it cradles your spirit with grace and enduring calm.

Affirmation: Calm surrounds and supports you, strengthening your spirit.

27th January
The Winter Breath

In the crisp embrace of a January dawn, where the air sparkles with the chill of winter, each breath you draw is a quiet gift, like the frost that gilds the bare branches of an elm. The field mouse, scurrying beneath the snow to its hidden nest, pulses with a life that echoes the steady rhythm within your chest. Along the frosty shore, the cormorant spreads its wings against the cold sea breeze, its calm defiance a mirror to your own enduring spirit. As you stand in this serene, wintry world, let the clear flow of a frozen brook, ever-moving beneath its icy veil, reflect the life that stirs within you. Each gentle inhale is a moment of renewal, like the owl gliding silently through the twilight, its presence felt but unseen. In this season of quiet frost and still air, your mindful breaths weave a thread of hope, grounding you in the present. Let this winter's breath guide you, for like the soft mist rising from a snowy valley, it carries the promise of resilience and calm.

Affirmation: Each breath fills you with calm, strength, and renewal.

28th January
Quiet Horizons

Though winter stretches wide, horizons remain, soft and open. Today, notice the possibilities ahead, however subtle. Each mindful step is a movement toward hope, each quiet thought a spark of courage. Even in stillness, you journey forward, carried by inner strength and gentle trust. Let your heart remain open, your mind attentive, and your spirit steady. The horizon is wide, welcoming, and full of light.

Affirmation: Your path is open, guided by quiet strength and hope.

29th January
Snowy Pathways

In the gentle quiet of a January morning, where snow dusts the paths through meadow and wood, each step you take resonates with the steady pulse of winter, like the ancient holly standing firm against the cold. The stoat, weaving its nimble trail through the frosted undergrowth, carries a spark of life that mirrors your own quiet determination. As you tread these snowy pathways, let the crunch of frost beneath your feet echo the clarity within your mind, grounding you in the present. Each pause for breath is a moment of warmth, like the hare resting in its snowy form, safe in the stillness. In this season of crisp air and muffled light, your every step is a gentle triumph, weaving hope through the frosted world. Let this winter's path guide you, for like the faint glow of dawn on a snowy hill, it shines with the promise of endurance and calm.

Affirmation: You move forward with grace, strength, and quiet courage.

30th January
The Gift of Presence

Today, be present in the small, subtle moments — the quiet of a room, the shimmer of frost, the softness of a breath. Each act of presence is a gift to yourself, strengthening your spirit and nurturing calm. Even amidst challenges, the act of noticing, pausing, and breathing fills your heart with peace. Let presence guide your steps, your thoughts, and your awareness, creating a sanctuary of inner calm and strength.

Affirmation: Being present nurtures your heart, mind, and spirit.

31st January — Monthly Reflection Poem
January's Quiet Dawn

Winter's hush has settled deep,
A tender calm the world will keep.
Snow lays soft on branch and ground,
A gentle quiet all around.
Your spirit, like the frost, shines clear,
Steady, patient, free from fear.
Each breath a thread of quiet light,
Carrying hope through the longest night.
Even in shadow, warmth endures,
Guided by courage that reassures.
Your heart, a lantern, softly glows,
Through frost, through stillness, it only grows.
Patience, resilience, calm, and care,
Are the quiet gifts you carry there.
Trust in this rhythm, slow and true,
January's light resides in you.

Affirmation: You carry hope, calm, and strength through every day, gently and enduringly.

FEBRUARY

1st February – Monthly Opening Poem

Gentle Awakening

February breathes a softer light,
Grey skies whisper, tender and bright.
Winter lingers, yet hints of thaw
Bring quiet hope, revealing awe.
Each breath you take is fresh and new,
A gentle strength flowing through you.
Though cold winds blow and skies are pale,
Your spirit carries a steadfast trail.
Soft buds hide beneath the frozen ground,
Whispering life waiting to be found.
Patience grows in each careful pause,
Resilience nurtures without a cause.
February calls with gentle grace,
And holds hope steady in your space.
Through frost, through quiet, through all you do,
Know strength and renewal belong to you.

Affirmation: You embrace the month with hope, calm, and gentle courage.

2nd February
The Soft Pulse of Life

Life continues gently beneath the frost, moving with a rhythm that is subtle yet steady. Today, notice your own inner pulse, the quiet strength that beats within. Even in moments of uncertainty, you are supported by this invisible current of resilience. Let each breath, each pause, each careful step remind you that life unfolds at its own pace. You are both witness and participant, guided by trust and gentle intention. The world may feel still, but your heart carries movement, hope, and calm.

Affirmation: Your heart carries strength, movement, and quiet hope.

3rd February
The Warmth Beneath Cold

In the crisp stillness of a February morning, where frost cloaks the rolling hills in a delicate sheen, nature holds a quiet beauty, like the ancient hawthorn standing steadfast against the winter's bite. The fox, with its russet coat glowing softly in the pale light, treads lightly across the frozen ground, its quiet steps a testament to life's enduring warmth. As you move through this chilled world, let the gentle glow of a frost-kissed meadow reflect the steady light within your heart. Each breath you take is a moment of calm, grounding you like the roots of an oak buried deep beneath the snow. In this season of cold air and hushed landscapes, your every pause weaves a thread of resilience, nurturing your spirit. Embrace this inner warmth, for like the faint shimmer of sunlight on a frosted branch, it guides you through the day with grace. Let this winter's quiet beauty remind you that your strength shines softly, ever-present beneath the cold.

Affirmation: You carry warmth and calm within you, always accessible.

4th February
The Gift of Presence

Notice the subtle rhythms of your day, the soft moments that often go unseen. Each breath, each glance, each gentle movement is an opportunity to be present. Today, let presence nurture your spirit and strengthen your patience. Even amidst challenges or fatigue, you are supported by the steady awareness of your own heart. Each small act of mindfulness, each quiet moment, affirms your inner strength and resilience.

Affirmation: Being present nurtures your spirit, strengthens your patience, and brings calm.

5th February
The Quiet Resilience

Resilience is not always loud; often, it is a gentle undercurrent that carries you through each day. Today, notice how even the smallest actions, pauses, and breaths build your strength. Every mindful step is a declaration of courage. Even when challenges feel heavy, your spirit moves with quiet determination. Trust in your enduring inner resources, letting them support your heart, your mind, and your body.

Affirmation: You move through challenges with quiet courage and steady strength.

6th February
The Whisper of Hope

In the tender hush of a February dawn, where the frosted fields glisten under a pale winter sky, nature murmurs a quiet promise, like the slender birch swaying gently in the chilly breeze. The red deer, stepping softly through the snow-dappled glade, carries a silent grace, its steady gaze a beacon of hope amidst the cold. As you wander through this serene, frosty world, let the delicate shimmer of ice on a frozen stream reflect the gentle spark within your soul. Each mindful breath you take is a moment of renewal, grounding you like the deep roots of an ancient yew. In this season of crisp air and quiet light, your every pause kindles a flame of hope, warming your spirit. Embrace this soft whisper, for like the faint glow of dawn breaking over a snowy hill, it guides your heart with gentle certainty. Let this winter's calm beauty remind you that hope endures, a steady light shining through even the coldest moments.

Affirmation: Hope whispers to you, guiding and sustaining your spirit.

7th February
The Winter Stream

Beneath the frost the stream still flows,
Quietly weaving where the cold wind blows.
Even when ice conceals its gleam,
Life continues, soft as a dream.
Your spirit moves with patient grace,
Each gentle step a sacred space.
Through silent mornings and muted light,
Strength grows quietly, steady and bright.
Each breath a ripple, each pause a wave,
Carrying hope, steady and brave.
Though winter lingers, the current remains,
Flowing through heart, through joys, through pains.
Trust its movement, tender and true,
It carries renewal and courage to you.
Let calm and patience guide your day,
And let the stream lead you on your way.

Affirmation: You move with gentle flow, guided by hope and quiet courage.

8th February
The Subtle Strength of Winter

In the quiet chill of a February morn, where frost adorns the meadows with a delicate sheen, nature holds a serene strength, like the steadfast willow bending gracefully by the frozen stream. The otter, gliding smoothly through the icy waters, weaves a dance of resilience, its sleek form a quiet testament to life's persistence in the cold. As you move through this frosted world, let the soft glint of sunlight on a frozen pond reflect the steady power within your heart. Each mindful breath you draw is a moment of calm, grounding you like the roots of an ancient elm beneath the snow. In this season of still air and gentle light, your every pause and gentle act kindles a spark of courage, warming your spirit. Embrace this subtle strength, for like the faint shimmer of dawn on an icy bank, it guides you with quiet hope. Let winter's calm beauty remind you that your inner light shines steadfast, even in the coldest moments.

Affirmation: You draw strength from within, quiet and steadfast.

9th February
Silver Light

Winter sunlight glints softly on frost and bare branches, illuminating even the smallest details. Today, let this silver light remind you of the quiet beauty and resilience in your own life. Each mindful pause, each careful step, is a gentle act of courage. Even amidst challenges, your inner light persists, illuminating your path. Notice it, nurture it, and allow it to guide you with calm assurance.

Affirmation: Your inner light shines steadily, guiding and comforting you.

10th February
The Flow of Quiet Moments

In the serene hush of a February day, where frost drapes the coastal cliffs in a delicate veil, nature whispers of quiet endurance, like the gentle ripples of a tide pool cradled by winter's chill. The seal, bobbing gracefully in the icy waves, moves with a steady rhythm, its sleek form a symbol of life's flow amidst the cold sea. As you pause in this frosty world, let the soft shimmer of light on a frozen estuary mirror the calm current within your soul. Each gentle breath you take is a moment of presence, grounding you like the roots of a windswept dune grass holding firm against the winter gales. In this season of muted light and crisp air, your every mindful step ripples with resilience, nurturing your spirit. Embrace these quiet moments, for like the faint glow of a winter moon on the tide, they guide your heart with subtle strength. Let this serene flow remind you that even in stillness, your inner vitality shines softly, ever-present.

Affirmation: You move gently through life, guided by presence and quiet strength.

11th February
The Gift of Patience

Patience is a soft companion, encouraging calm and trust in every moment. Today, let yourself move slowly, breathe deeply, and honour the unfolding of your journey. Even in waiting, there is growth, healing, and quiet triumph. Trust that each breath, each pause, and each mindful act contributes to your enduring resilience. Patience is not passive — it is a tender, sustaining strength that carries you forward.

Affirmation: Patience nurtures and strengthens your heart and spirit.

12th February
The Warmth Within

In the crisp embrace of a February dawn, where icy winds sweep across the coastal dunes, nature holds a quiet beauty, like the soft glow of dawn touching the frost-kissed shore. The harbour seal, resting on a rocky outcrop amidst the chilly waves, embodies a gentle resilience, its steady presence a beacon of warmth in the wintry sea. As you move through this frosted world, let the shimmer of light on a frozen tide pool reflect the quiet fire within your heart. Each mindful breath you draw is a moment of calm, grounding you like the sturdy reeds that stand firm against the coastal breeze. In this season of cold gusts and muted light, your every pause kindles a spark of courage, nurturing your spirit. Embrace this inner warmth, for like the faint glow of a lighthouse beam cutting through the winter mist, it guides you with gentle grace. Let this serene radiance remind you that your strength shines softly, even in the coldest moments.

Affirmation: You carry steady warmth and calm within you.

13th February
The Gentle Light of Hope

Even on grey winter days, hope glimmers quietly, subtle and persistent. Today, notice its presence within you — a soft glow guiding your heart, thoughts, and actions. Each breath, each pause, each gentle step is an act of trust in your resilience. Even when challenges feel heavy, hope endures, illuminating your path and sustaining your spirit. Let it rise softly within you, a faithful companion through every moment.

Affirmation: Hope rises gently within you, steady and true.

14th February
The Lanterns of Winter

Lanterns glow along snowy lanes,
Soft circles of warmth that light remains.
Though winter winds may bite and blow,
Each lantern glimmers with steady glow.
Your heart is a lantern, steadfast and bright,
Guiding you through the longest night.
Each mindful thought, each gentle breath,
Carries hope, courage, and life beneath.
Even in shadows, the flame persists,
A quiet companion that never quits.
Step softly into its warming light,
Let patience guide you through the night.
Trust in its presence, tender and true,
It carries renewal, strength, and you.
Through frost, through silence, through skies of grey,
Your inner light illuminates the way.

Affirmation: Your inner light guides you with warmth, hope, and courage.

15th February
The Flow of Winter Days

Winter days stretch long, yet within each moment there is gentle opportunity. Today, notice the subtle rhythm of your breath, the quiet resilience of your heart, and the small acts of care that sustain you. Even amidst challenges, your spirit carries calm, patience, and hope. Let the gentle flow of your day remind you that strength grows quietly, often in ways unseen but always felt.

Affirmation: You move through winter with quiet strength and calm presence.

16th February
The Frosted Horizon

Look ahead and notice the soft light touching the horizon, even amidst frost and cold. Today, let this subtle illumination remind you of possibilities, gentle hope, and resilience. Each breath and step carries you forward, strengthening your heart and mind. Even small, mindful acts are victories, quiet yet profound. Trust in the unfolding of your path, guided by calm, courage, and patience.

Affirmation: You are guided by hope, courage, and gentle trust.

17th February
The Subtle Courage

In the soft stillness of a February morn, where frost weaves a delicate lace across the rolling fields, nature whispers of quiet fortitude, like the steadfast ash standing tall against the winter's chill. The hare, with its gentle bounds across the snow-dusted meadow, carries a subtle bravery, its quiet movements a testament to life's enduring spirit. As you tread through this frosted world, let the faint glimmer of sunlight on icy branches reflect the steady courage within your heart. Each deliberate breath you take is a moment of strength, grounding you like the deep roots of an ancient tree beneath the frozen earth. In this season of crisp air and hushed landscapes, your every soft step weaves a thread of resilience, nurturing your soul. Embrace this quiet courage, for like the pale glow of dawn on a snowy path, it guides you with gentle resolve. Let this winter's serene beauty remind you that your bravery shines softly, steadfast even in the coldest hours.

Affirmation: Your courage is steady, quiet, and enduring.

18th February
The Winter Garden

Even in winter, the world holds hidden beauty — frost on branches, soft snow, and quiet light. Today, notice the small wonders around you, allowing them to lift your heart and spirit. Each mindful observation, each pause for reflection, is nourishment for your resilience. Though the season is cold, your heart blooms softly with hope, patience, and quiet joy.

Affirmation: You notice and cherish the quiet beauty in your world.

19th February
The Winter Hearth

A fire glows against the winter night,
Its warmth a comfort, steady and bright.
Though frost may bite and winds may howl,
Its gentle light holds calm and soul.
Your heart, a hearth, carries steady flame,
Guiding your spirit, whispering your name.
Each breath you take fans the gentle glow,
Through quiet rooms and soft white snow.
Even in stillness, warmth persists,
A soft reminder that hope exists.
Step near, feel its steady embrace,
Let patience and courage shape your space.
Through long nights, through shadows deep,
Its light endures, its promise keeps.
Trust in this flame, tender and true,
It carries renewal, hope, and you.

Affirmation: Your inner warmth guides you with hope, calm, and courage.

20th February
The Gentle Rhythm

Pause and breathe in this February morning, where frost-kissed meadows glow softly under a pale winter sky, and nature hums a quiet melody, like the steadfast oak standing tall through the season's chill. The badger, ambling gently through the snow-draped undergrowth, moves with a steady rhythm, its unhurried steps echoing the calm pulse within your heart. Feel each breath you draw, weaving a thread of resilience, like the faint ripples of a frozen stream locked beneath its icy surface. In this season of hushed light and crisp air, your every heartbeat mirrors the quiet strength of the earth, grounding you in the present. Each mindful pause is a tender act of care, warming your spirit like sunlight piercing a winter cloud. Let this gentle rhythm guide your day, for it shines with the soft glow of hope, steady and true. Trust in its flow, as it carries you through each moment with grace.

Affirmation: You move through life with steady, gentle rhythm.

21st February
The Whispering Wind

Step gently into this February morning, where the winter winds weave through the frost-laden trees, and nature sings a quiet hymn, like the bare branches of a sycamore swaying in the breeze. The wren, flitting swiftly through the snowy hedgerows, carries a delicate courage, its tiny form a beacon of resilience against the gusts. Feel each breath you take, steadying your heart like the soft ripples of a frozen lake touched by the wind's fleeting caress. In this season of crisp air and fleeting light, your every mindful step echoes the calm strength of the earth, grounding you amidst the storm. Each pause you take is a quiet act of fortitude, warming your spirit like the faint glow of dawn breaking through a clouded sky. Let the whispering wind guide your day, for it carries the soft promise of endurance, steady and true. Trust in this inner stillness, as it holds you firm with grace through winter's restless dance.

Affirmation: You are steady, strong, and resilient in every moment.

22nd February
The Light Within

Even when the skies are grey, your inner light remains, persistent and luminous. Today, allow it to guide your actions, thoughts, and presence. Each small, mindful act is a reflection of that light, carrying hope, patience, and calm. Trust this steady flame within, and let it illuminate your journey.

Affirmation: Your inner light shines steadily, guiding and comforting you.

23rd February
The Soft Strength

Strength is often quiet, a subtle current beneath the surface of life. Today, notice your own gentle power — the resilience that endures, the courage that persists, and the calm that flows. Each mindful breath, each small pause, is an affirmation of this enduring strength. Even when challenges feel heavy, you are supported by the quiet power within.

Affirmation: Your quiet strength carries you gently through every day.

24th February
The Winter Path

Through snowed-in paths and frost-bound lanes,
Life flows gently, despite the chains.
Your steps are careful, soft, and true,
Each one guided by the light in you.
Though winter lingers and skies are pale,
Your spirit moves, steady and hale.
Each mindful act, each patient breath,
Builds resilience, life, and quiet depth.
Even in stillness, you journey far,
Guided by courage, hope, and heart's star.
Step lightly through the frozen day,
Let patience and calm light your way.
Trust the rhythm, slow and bright,
Winter carries renewal and light.
Through long nights, through quiet skies,
Your inner strength and hope arise.

Affirmation: You move steadily with hope, courage, and quiet grace.

25th February
The Pause of Reflection

Beneath the pale February sky, where frost clings to the gnarled branches of an ancient hawthorn, the world holds its breath in a moment of quiet reverence. The blackbird, perched silently on a snow-dusted bough, gazes over the frozen fields, its stillness a mirror to the gentle courage within you. In this serene winter light, each pause you take reflects the soft shimmer of a frosted meadow, grounding your spirit in the present. Your every breath carries the steady rhythm of the earth, like the faint pulse of life beneath the icy soil. As you rest in these moments of reflection, feel the calm strength that grows within, warming your heart like the first hint of sunlight on a chilly morn. This season of crisp air and muted hues invites you to honour your journey, each small step a testament to resilience. Let this quiet pause, like the blackbird's watchful gaze, fill you with patience and grace, guiding you gently forward.

Affirmation: Reflection strengthens and nurtures your spirit.

26th February
The Tender Horizon

Notice the horizon, soft and pale, hinting at possibilities beyond the winter grey. Today, let this subtle promise inspire gentle hope. Each mindful breath, each careful step, carries you closer to renewal and growth. Even amidst challenges, your spirit moves with patience and courage. Trust in this unfolding, and let gentle awareness guide your heart.

Affirmation: You trust in the gentle unfolding of your path.

27th February
The Gentle Flow

Life moves with a quiet persistence, much like a stream stirring beneath winter's fading ice, preparing itself for the greening days of March. Beneath stillness, there is always motion, a tender rhythm guiding you onwards even when unseen. Today, let yourself attune to those hidden currents—the unspoken thoughts, the subtle emotions, the steady pulse of your own being. Each small gesture of kindness, each patient breath, is part of this gentle tide of resilience, carrying you through both shadow and light. Picture the hare, poised at the field's edge, sensing the stirrings of spring; its alert stillness reminds us that movement does not always mean haste. In the same way, your path unfolds quietly, with grace and assurance. Trust this steady flow, for it knows how to lead you into calmer waters and brighter days.

Affirmation: You flow with life gently, guided by patience and hope.

28th February
The Quiet Bloom

Even in winter's chill, quiet growth occurs. Today, notice the small ways you are blooming — in thought, in breath, in heart. Each mindful moment nurtures this quiet resilience, reminding you that life continues, gently but persistently. Let your awareness celebrate these subtle victories.

Affirmation: You nurture gentle growth and resilience in yourself.

29th February — Monthly Reflection Poem
February's Gentle Bloom

Winter lingers, soft and still,
Yet subtle blooms obey their will.
Your spirit, quiet, steady, bright,
Carries hope through each long night.
Each breath, each pause, each gentle step,
Reveals the strength you quietly kept.
Even amidst frost and muted skies,
Your heart endures, patient and wise.
Through shadows, through winds, through silent days,
Resilience flows in calm, steady ways.
Trust the rhythm, tender and true,
February holds gentle renewal for you.
Let patience, hope, and quiet light
Guide every moment, morning to night.
Your inner courage, soft yet strong,
Carries you gently your whole life long.

Affirmation: You carry hope, resilience, and quiet courage through every day.

MARCH

1st March – Monthly Opening Poem

Awakening Light

March arrives with softening skies,
Hints of warmth in the sun's rise.
Snowdrops bow, yet bravely stand,
Whispering hope across the land.
The air is crisp, the earth still sleeps,
Yet hidden life beneath it keeps.
Each breath you take, each mindful pause,
Holds renewal without a cause.
Even in chill, the world prepares,
For buds to break and life declares.
Let patience guide your quiet heart,
As winter's end and spring impart.
March calls gently with subtle cheer,
And carries hope that you hold dear.
Trust the rhythm, soft and true,
This month's light belongs to you.

Affirmation: You welcome the quiet strength of renewal and grow in harmony with the rhythm of life, carrying hope gently into all you do.

2nd March
The Soft Light of Dawn

Morning light spills golden across the horizon, where robins trill softly in bare branches. Today, let its warmth cradle your thoughts, heart, and every breath you take. Amid the lingering chill, find promise in each mindful pause and deliberate step. This gentle glow nurtures your spirit, offering a beacon of calm amid the cold. The rhythm of birds stirring and trees standing tall inspires courage and quiet joy. Take a moment to absorb this serenity, letting it weave through your day's journey. Feel the light renew your inner strength, a soft promise of brighter days ahead.

Affirmation: The dawn's light fills you with serenity, hope, and inner strength.

3rd March
The Whisper of Growth

Beneath the frost, life gathers strength, echoed by the swift movement of a fox through the undergrowth, and today you can listen to these whispers—buds swelling, streams thawing—as they stir your soul, letting each mindful moment nurture your resilience, a quiet force building within. Even in the coldest times, progress hums unseen, a testament to your enduring spirit, so trust your heart's steady preparation for renewal, carrying hope and courage forward, and allow this gentle awakening to guide your steps, offering peace in its subtle rhythm while feeling the earth's quiet pulse align with your own, fostering strength for the days to come.

Affirmation: You cultivate growth and resilience with every conscious breath.

4th March
The Gentle March of Time

Time flows like wind through bare oaks, a soft cadence to your days' unfolding, and today you can feel its rhythm in your breath and steps, each a testament to quiet courage, advancing with graceful, patient resolve amid uncertainty or weariness. Let the gentle hours bring reflection and trust, sowing seeds of hope in your heart's fertile ground, where each moment holds meaning, and embrace this slow dance of time, allowing it to steady your soul with calm assurance, knowing every step forward is a victory, guided by your inner wisdom.

Affirmation: You progress steadily, led by patience, courage, and inner wisdom.

5th March
The Strength of Quiet Moments

In the stillness of morning, strength gathers like dew on spider webs, mirrored by squirrels pausing in the trees, and today you can rest and reflect, letting each mindful act—deep breaths, soft smiles—nurture your spirit like early shoots rising through thawing soil, where your resilience grows with steady grace. Each quiet moment weaves renewal and peace, a sanctuary amid life's challenges, so trust this stillness to replenish your energy, offering a gentle embrace to your heart, and allow the serenity of these pauses to guide you, fostering courage for the day ahead while feeling the strength within you deepen, a quiet power ready to carry you forward.

Affirmation: Your strength blossoms quietly, sustained by calm, hope, and presence.

6th March
The Promise in the Breeze

Feel the wind brush the hedgerows, where hares hint at warmth to come, a whisper of renewal, and today you can let this gentle breeze assure you that change and hope are drawing near, with each mindful breath and step unfolding with patience. Even in cold stillness, trust life's currents to guide you with calm and certainty, your heart holding steadfast courage, and let this subtle movement inspire your spirit, filling it with peaceful anticipation while embracing the promise carried on the wind, knowing it nurtures your soul's growth.

Affirmation: You embrace life's unfolding with hope and gentle fortitude.

7th March
The Thawing Stream

A stream glimmers beneath melting snow,
Its waters whisper as they softly flow.
Though winter lingers with frost and grey,
Life stirs quietly, finding its way.
Your spirit moves like this gentle stream,
Steady and calm, embracing each dream.
Each breath you take, a ripple of light,
Each mindful pause, a current bright.
Even in shadow, hope persists,
Guided by courage that quietly insists.
Step softly along this thawing flow,
Let patience and trust guide you as you go.
Though winds may chill and clouds may hide,
Your inner strength remains at your side.
Trust in the stream, its rhythm true,
It carries calm, renewal, and you.

Affirmation: Your inner currents carry hope, calm, and quiet courage.

8th March
The Quiet Bud

The earth half-dreams, yet tender buds stir beneath, as dormice nestle in hidden hollows, and today you can sense your own quiet growth, the pulse of resilience carrying you forth, with each mindful breath and gentle act nurturing your spirit like sun coaxing life from winter. Trust patience to guide you, allowing courage to bloom unseen within your heart, and let this subtle strength steady your steps, a quiet promise of renewal to come while feeling the earth's tender awakening resonate with your own, fostering hope and calm, knowing this inner bud is growing, ready to flourish with time and care.

Affirmation: Your inner growth fosters hope, courage, and renewal.

9th March
The Soft Hum of Life

Listen to the lark's song rising, the wind rustling through bare elms—a hum of persistence, and today you can let these sounds reflect your spirit's quiet energy, moving with purpose and grace, with each mindful breath reaffirming your strength even when days weigh heavy with challenge. Life thrives beneath the frost, a mirror to your own enduring resilience, so trust this rhythm to fill you with calm, hope, and a gentle joy that lifts your soul, allowing the natural symphony to guide your thoughts, offering peace in every moment while feeling this soft hum align with your heartbeat, a reminder of life's quiet strength.

Affirmation: You align with life's gentle rhythm, guided by hope and strength.

10th March
The Gentle Stirring

Mark the light's subtle shift, a warm touch on your skin as badgers emerge at dusk, and today you can let these signs of change remind you that renewal is steadily approaching, with each pause and breath carrying courage and patience. Amid cold or doubt, trust your heart's quiet advance, like shoots pushing through soil, strong and unseen, and let this stirring inspire your spirit, filling it with hope for the days ahead while feeling the earth's awakening echo in your soul, guiding you with tender assurance and embracing this gradual shift, knowing your resilience grows steadily.

Affirmation: You welcome change with patience, courage, and hope.

11th March
The Strength in Stillness

In stillness, find strength, as deer stand poised in the morning mist, a picture of calm, and today you can let your breath bridge you to serenity, a reminder of your deep resilience, with each pause nourishing your spirit and steadying your heart as the days gently lengthen. Amid challenges, trust patience and presence to guide you toward renewal's promise, allowing this quiet strength to envelop you, offering a peaceful refuge within, and feel your spirit stir softly, ready to embrace the growth that lies ahead, knowing this stillness is your ally, fostering courage for every step forward.

Affirmation: Your inner strength is steadfast, serene, and enduring.

12th March
The First Sunlight

Morning light filters through oaks, tender and gold, as finches flit in the branches, and today you can let it fill your heart and breath, warming your spirit like frost-kissed earth, with each mindful step nurturing courage. Trust this soft light to guide you with hope and calm, renewal ever near, and feel its gentle touch soothe your soul, a beacon through any lingering chill, allowing this illumination to inspire your day, lifting your spirits with peace and knowing this sunlight mirrors your inner light, growing brighter with each moment.

Affirmation: You are guided by the tender light of hope, courage, and peace.

13th March
The Whisper of Growth

Beneath still soil, life readies to rise, as moles tunnel in the dark earth with purpose, and today you can notice your strength's quiet growth, with each breath and act a sign of progress amid cold or uncertainty. Trust your spirit's persistent stir, carrying hope and courage like shoots awaiting sun, and let these subtle whispers guide your heart, fostering resilience while feeling the earth's hidden energy resonate with your own, a promise of renewal, allowing this gentle progress to steady your soul and offering peace in its quiet rhythm, knowing your resilience is building, ready to bloom with patient care.

Affirmation: Your growth is patient, persistent, and quietly powerful.

14th March
The Early Spring Stream

A stream glimmers under melting frost,
Its waters flowing, no matter the cost.
Though winter lingers with lingering chill,
Life moves gently, persistent, still.
Your spirit flows like this thawing stream,
Calm and steady, embracing each dream.
Each mindful pause, each thoughtful breath,
Carries resilience, hope, and depth.
Even when skies are muted and grey,
Strength and courage continue their way.
Step softly into this gentle flow,
Let patience and trust guide you as you go.
Though challenges linger and winds may bite,
Your inner calm remains steadfast and bright.
Trust the current, tender and true,
It carries renewal, light, and you.

Affirmation: You flow with quiet courage, guided by hope and steady strength.

15th March
The Subtle Bloom

See green threading hedgerows, crocuses lifting through frost, as hedgehogs stir from hibernation, and today you can let these signs mirror your resilience, a quiet strength within your soul, with each mindful breath nurturing courage even in stillness. Trust these subtle blooms to guide you, your heart flourishing with patience and hope, and feel the earth's tender awakening echo in your being, offering a sense of calm while allowing this gentle progress to inspire your day, filling it with peaceful resolve and knowing your resilience mirrors nature's quiet beauty, ready to thrive in time.

Affirmation: You tend your resilience with gentleness, patience, and fortitude.

16th March
The Gentle Wind

Feel the wind brush your face, carrying the scent of earth as otters glide in thawing streams, and today you can let it remind you life moves subtly, a gentle force shaping your journey, with each breath and pause carrying courage. Like the wind sculpting winter's remnants, your spirit persists, weaving hope and calm into every moment, so trust this soft movement to guide your heart, offering a sense of serene progress, and allow the wind's whisper to lift your spirits, fostering strength within your soul while feeling its gentle touch align with your resilience, a promise of renewal ahead.

Affirmation: You advance with courage, hope, and quiet resolve.

17th March
The Strength of Patience

Like buds awaiting spring sun, your strength unfolds, as stoats dart through the underbrush, and today you can let patience guide your heart, with each breath and act nurturing your resilience though progress hides beneath the surface. Trust your spirit's quiet, steady growth, mirroring nature's gentle rhythm, and feel the earth's patient energy resonate within you, bringing peace to your soul while allowing this strength to steady your steps, a quiet power building with each day and knowing your heart is blossoming, guided by the calm wisdom of time.

Affirmation: Your patience fortifies your heart and nurtures your spirit.

18th March
The Light on Frost

Sun glints on frost-laden branches, as wrens sing in the chill, a fleeting spark of beauty, and today you can let it remind you of hope amid the cold, a light within your reach, with each mindful pause nurturing strength. Trust that light persists within and around you, guiding your thoughts with calm, and feel this gentle illumination warm your soul, offering peace amid the frost while allowing its sparkle to inspire your day, lifting your spirit with hopeful grace and knowing this light reflects your inner resilience, shining steadily onward.

Affirmation: You cherish and embrace the light of hope and resilience.

19th March
The Awakening Wood

A wood stirs under pale winter skies,
Soft buds swelling, unseen by eyes.
Though frost still grips the sleeping ground,
Quiet strength and hope abound.
Your spirit moves like this gentle wood,
Steadily, calmly, as you should.
Each mindful breath, each gentle step,
Nurtures courage and the dreams you kept.
Even in stillness, life prepares,
For days of warmth, sun, and cares.
Step softly into the awakening light,
Let patience guide you, tender and bright.
Though chill may linger and clouds may stay,
Your inner warmth will show the way.
Trust this rhythm, gentle and true,
It carries renewal, hope, and you.

Affirmation: Your heart awakens with calm, courage, and quiet strength.

20th March
The First Soft Green

Faint green graces hedgerows, shy as rabbits in the dawn, a tender sign of renewal, and today you can let it mirror your courage, a quiet force stirring within your soul, with each breath nurturing resilience even in quiet moments. Trust life's gradual unfolding, your heart flourishing with patience and hope, and feel the earth's gentle awakening resonate with your own, bringing calm and strength while allowing this soft green to guide your day, filling it with peaceful anticipation and knowing your growth mirrors nature's quiet beauty, blossoming with time.

Affirmation: You foster your growth with patience, hope, and quiet resilience.

21st March
The Gentle Thaw

Winter's chill softens as streams stir, otters gliding beneath melting ice with grace, and today you can notice nature's gentle motion—wind, light, the rhythm of your own breath—with each step carrying courage. Trust your spirit's steady flow, embracing change with a peaceful heart, and feel the earth's thawing energy align with your soul, offering hope and calm while allowing this subtle shift to inspire your day, guiding you with gentle resolve and knowing your resilience flows like the streams, steady and enduring.

Affirmation: You progress with calm, courage, and gentle endurance.

22nd March
Horizon of Gentle Growth

The horizon glows with early spring light, as deer graze in the distance with quiet dignity, and today you can let it fill your heart with hope and patience, a soft promise of growth, with each breath strengthening your courage. Trust your steady inner growth, your heart awakening to bloom in its own time, and feel this tender light soothe your spirit, offering peace amid the day's journey while allowing it to guide your thoughts, lifting you with a sense of gentle purpose and knowing your soul mirrors this horizon, expanding with each mindful moment.

Affirmation: Your heart stirs with hope, patience, and quiet bravery.

23rd March
The Whispering Branches

Bare branches sway, rooks nesting with grace, a testament to nature's persistence, and today you can let them reflect your resilience, bending but never breaking under strain, with each pause expressing strength. Amid uncertainty, your spirit stands tall, rooted in hope, a steady presence through every challenge, and feel the branches' gentle movement resonate with your own heart's rhythm while allowing their whisper to guide your day, filling it with calm and resolve and knowing your strength grows deep, nourished by the earth's quiet wisdom.

Affirmation: You are resilient, steadfast, and enduring in every moment.

24th March
The Thawing Meadow

A meadow stirs beneath frost's retreat,
Soft shoots pushing through earth beneath your feet.
Though winter lingers with muted skies,
Life awakens, quiet and wise.
Your spirit moves like this gentle land,
Calm, patient, guided by steady hand.
Each mindful breath, each thoughtful pause,
Carries courage and quiet cause.
Even in shadow, hope persists,
Strength and calm quietly insist.
Step softly into this tender day,
Let inner wisdom guide your way.
Though chill remains and winds may bite,
Your gentle heart carries light.
Trust the meadow, tender and true,
It blooms with patience, hope, and you.

Affirmation: Your inner courage blooms quietly, guiding you through change.

25th March
The Flow of Life

Life flows like a stream under the sun, as salmon leap in the current with purpose, and today you can feel your breath's rhythm, your heart's pulse, a gentle tide within you, with each step carrying hope. Even in stillness, trust this flow to guide your thoughts, actions, and heart, and let the stream's energy inspire your soul, offering a sense of calm progression while allowing its movement to fill your day, nurturing peace and resilience within and knowing your spirit flows steadily, carried by hope's gentle current.

Affirmation: You journey through life with steady calm, hope, and strength.

26th March
The Warmth of the Sun

Sun pierces clouds, warming the earth, as butterflies flutter near crocuses with delicate grace, and today you can let its light fill your heart with hope, a gentle warmth for your soul, with each breath nurturing resilience. Trust your spirit's steady progress, guided by this soft, renewing energy, and feel the sun's touch soothe your spirit, offering peace amid the day's flow while allowing its warmth to inspire your steps, lifting you with gentle courage and knowing this light mirrors your inner glow, shining brighter with each moment.

Affirmation: The sun's gentle warmth nurtures your heart and spirit.

27th March
The First Bees

Hear bees hum over crocus blooms, a persistent dance of spring with quiet purpose, and today you can let them inspire your perseverance, a steady force within your soul, with each act nurturing strength. Amid fatigue, trust life's persistent pulse, your heart tending renewal, and feel their gentle hum resonate with your spirit, offering hope and calm while allowing this sound to guide your day, filling it with peaceful determination and knowing your resilience grows, nurtured by nature's quiet harmony.

Affirmation: You persist with care, nurturing your spirit with hope and resilience.

28th March
The Early Spring Garden

A garden wakes beneath pale light,
Soft shoots emerge from winter's night.
Though frost may linger and skies are grey,
Life stirs gently, finding its way.
Your heart blooms like this tender land,
Steady, patient, guided by your hand.
Each mindful breath, each thoughtful act,
Nurtures courage and hope intact.
Even in shadow, life prepares,
For warmth, for growth, and open airs.
Step softly into this quiet scene,
Let patience and trust guide what's unseen.
Though chill remains and clouds may stay,
Your inner strength will light your way.
Trust the garden, tender and true,
It blooms with patience, hope, and you.

Affirmation: Your heart blooms quietly, nurtured by patience and hope.

29th March
The Gentle Breeze

A breeze caresses your skin, carrying earth's scent as hares bound in the fields with joy, and today you can let it signal change's quiet approach, a whisper of renewal in the air, with each pause nurturing resilience. Trust life's unfolding, your spirit awakening to bloom with gentle grace, and feel the breeze's touch align with your soul, offering peace and hope while allowing its movement to guide your day, filling it with calm anticipation and knowing your heart mirrors this breeze, growing stronger with each breath.

Affirmation: You flow gently with life, guided by calm, hope, and quiet courage.

30th March
The Soft Earth

Feel the soft earth beneath you, a cradle for growth as worms turn the soil with care, and today you can let it ground your resilience, a foundation for your inner strength, with each breath cultivating hope. Trust this rhythm, your courage blooming like seeds beneath the surface, and feel the earth's tender energy resonate with your spirit, offering calm and stability while allowing this grounding presence to guide your day, nurturing peace and growth and knowing your resilience takes root here, ready to flourish in its own time.

Affirmation: You are rooted, resilient, and growing with patience and hope.

31st March — Monthly Reflection Poem
March's Gentle Awakening

The earth awakens beneath soft skies,
Tender shoots lifting where frost still lies.
Your heart, like the soil, has rested and stirred,
Nurtured by patience, hope, and each word.
Each breath, each pause, each mindful act,
Carries resilience, courage, and quiet impact.
Though winter lingers and winds may chill,
Your inner strength moves steadily, still.
Step softly into this gentle light,
Let renewal guide you day and night.
Through quiet moments, through gentle days,
Hope blooms softly in tender ways.
Trust the rhythm, patient and true,
March carries calm, renewal, and you.
Your spirit awakens, gentle and strong,
Guided by courage all month long.

Affirmation: You carry patience, hope, and quiet courage through every day.

APRIL

1st April – Monthly Opening Poem

The Breath of Spring

April arrives with softer skies,
Clouds drifting lightly, sun's gentle rise.
Blossoms swell on branches bare,
A tender promise fills the air.
The earth is moist, alive, and new,
Each drop of rain a whispered cue.
Even in chill or sudden storm,
Life prepares its vibrant form.
Each mindful breath, each gentle step,
Carries hope your heart has kept.
Trust the rhythm of this month's flow,
Let quiet courage help you grow.
April whispers softly, calm and true,
"I hold patience, hope, and strength for you."

Affirmation: You welcome renewal, hope, and gentle courage this April.

2nd April
The Stirring Green

Look for tender shoots breaking through the soil, small yet persistent. Today, let these subtle signs of life mirror your own resilience. Each mindful breath and thoughtful pause strengthens your inner calm. Even in moments of uncertainty, your spirit moves forward, quietly preparing for growth. Trust the slow unfolding of your own strength, like the world around you awakening to spring. Let the gentle stir of life inspire your heart with patience and courage.

Affirmation: You grow quietly, nurtured by hope, patience, and courage.

3rd April
The Soft Breeze

Feel the breeze drifting lightly through budding trees, soft and playful. Today, let it carry away tension and worry, leaving calm and presence behind. Each breath and gentle movement nurtures resilience, strength, and hope. Even in quiet or challenging moments, trust in the steady flow of life. Allow the air's gentle caress to remind you that your heart, like nature, moves with purpose and calm.

Affirmation: You flow gently through life, guided by calm, hope, and resilience.

4th April
The Light Through Clouds

Notice how the April sun breaks through drifting clouds, its brightness softened by veils of grey, yet still it warms the earth with quiet persistence. Today, allow that tender light to seep into your own heart, offering hope where weariness lingers and warmth where shadows have gathered. Each mindful gesture, each steady step forward, becomes a way of leaning towards the light, nurturing resilience as surely as spring nurtures blossom. Even when days stretch slowly or skies feel heavy, trust that your spirit carries a radiance that cannot be dimmed. Think of the swallow returning from its long journey, slicing the air with graceful certainty—it reminds us that light and renewal always return, no matter the distance or delay. Like the sun through cloud, your inner strength pierces doubt with patience, preparing you gently for the season of growth ahead.

Affirmation: Your heart shines quietly, filled with hope, strength, and calm.

5th April
The First Blossom

Look closely at the first blossom on a tree or bush, fragile yet persistent. Today, let it remind you that even small signs of growth carry great meaning. Each breath, each pause, each act of care strengthens your spirit. Even amidst uncertainty or lingering fatigue, trust in the slow, gentle process of renewal. Your heart, like these early blooms, opens softly with patience and courage.

Affirmation: You embrace each small moment of growth with hope and calm.

6th April
The Gentle Earth

Feel the soil beneath your feet, softened by April's sun and stirred by the breath of spring. In its quiet warmth lies a reminder of your own resilience—steady, patient, and deeply rooted. Each mindful act, each thoughtful pause, is like a seed pressed gently into the ground, held in trust until its time to flourish arrives. Even in stillness, growth is taking place; your spirit stretches unseen, gathering strength beneath the surface of daily life. Think of the hedgehog emerging from its winter rest, tentative yet assured, moving in rhythm with the earth's renewal. Just as the land quietly sustains new life, so too does your inner ground hold the promise of calm and renewal. Trust in this gentle rhythm; it knows the way forward.

Affirmation: You are grounded, resilient, and quietly growing with patience and hope.

7th April
The Awakening Meadow

A meadow stirs beneath soft skies,
Tender shoots pushing where frost still lies.
Though winter's chill may linger near,
Life awakens with courage clear.
Your heart, like soil, has rested and stirred,
Nurtured by patience, hope, and each word.
Each mindful breath, each gentle pause,
Carries strength and quiet cause.
Even in shadow, life prepares,
For warmth, for blooms, and tender cares.
Step softly into this early light,
Let renewal guide your day and night.
Though chill remains and winds may bite,
Your inner calm shines steady and bright.
Trust the meadow, tender and true,
It blooms with hope, courage, and you.

Affirmation: Your heart awakens with calm, hope, and gentle strength.

8th April
The Thawing Stream

Notice the soft gurgle of a stream as ice melts and water flows again. Today, let this gentle movement remind you that life continues, even when change is slow or hidden. Each mindful breath and careful step nurtures calm, courage, and resilience. Like water carving its quiet path, your spirit moves steadily, shaping hope and renewal with every moment. Trust the currents of your heart, and let them guide you gently through the day.

Affirmation: Your spirit flows quietly, carrying hope, calm, and courage.

9th April
The Sun-Warmed Soil

Feel the sun as it tenderly warms the soil, loosening what was once hard, making way for roots to stretch and life to begin again. Let this quiet heat remind you of your own strength—gentle yet enduring, always preparing the ground for growth. Each mindful pause, each small act of kindness towards yourself or others, is like water seeping into the earth, nourishing what is yet unseen. Even in times of uncertainty or weariness, your spirit is gathering itself, drawing courage and calm from hidden reserves. Think of the blackbird turning the soil with its beak, seeking sustenance while unknowingly stirring seeds towards the light—so too do your simple actions help awaken new beginnings within. Trust this warming, trust this slow renewal; your heart, like the earth, is quietly readying itself for new life.

Affirmation: Your inner strength grows quietly, nurtured by calm, hope, and patience.

10th April
The Song of Birds

Listen to birds singing as they greet the morning light. Today, let their persistent melodies inspire your own quiet courage. Each breath, each mindful pause, carries resilience and hope. Even amidst challenges, your heart sings softly with strength. Like the birds returning after winter, your spirit rises steadily, patient and unwavering. Allow this gentle song to fill your mind and heart with calm and optimism.

Affirmation: Your spirit sings quietly, guided by patience, courage, and hope.

11th April
The First Wildflowers

See how the first wildflowers press through grass and earth, their fragile petals trembling in the spring breeze, yet their roots hold firm in quiet strength. Renewal often begins this way—softly, almost unnoticed—until one day colour spills across the fields and reminds us of life's persistence. Today, let these tender blooms guide you, showing that resilience is not always loud but often gentle, unfolding with patience. Each mindful act, each deliberate breath, is like sunlight upon the soil, coaxing forth hidden possibilities. Even when days feel long or edged with uncertainty, your own spirit is stirring, preparing to unfurl with quiet courage. Think of the honeybee hovering close, drawn to the blossoms' offering; it teaches us that even the smallest beginnings can nourish and sustain. Like the wildflowers, your heart opens slowly yet surely, carrying within it the promise of hope and renewal.

Affirmation: You embrace each small sign of growth with hope and quiet strength.

12th April
The Gentle Rainfall

Hear the rain falling softly, tapping leaves and earth with tender rhythm. Today, let each drop remind you that even small, quiet moments of care nurture your spirit. Each breath, each pause, each thoughtful action strengthens resilience and calm. Even in grey or challenging hours, trust that life persists and that your heart grows steadily. Allow the gentle rhythm of the rain to guide your thoughts, heart, and spirit toward renewal.

Affirmation: You are nurtured by gentle moments, patience, and quiet courage.

13th April
The Fresh Breeze

Feel the cool breeze as it brushes across your skin, carrying with it the scent of damp earth and the promise of awakening buds. Change often comes like this— softly, almost unnoticed at first, yet t shapes everything it touches. Today, let the air remind you that movement does not need to be fierce to be true; even the gentlest current carries you forwarc. Each mindful pause, each steady step, becomes part of this quiet rhythm, nurturing both courage and calm. Think of the lark rising on the wind, its wings lifted with ease, its song carried high above the fields; it shows us how trust in the air beneath can turn stillness into flight. So too does your heart move gently toward growth, renewal, and balance. Allow this fresh breeze to lift your spirit, clearing doubt, and steadying your mind with its tender strength.

Affirmation: You move with life's gentle rhythm, guided by hope and calm.

14th April
The Spring Garden

A garden wakes beneath soft skies,
Tender buds lifting where frost still lies.
Though winter's chill may linger near,
Life returns with courage clear.
Your spirit moves like this gentle land,
Steady, patient, guided by your hand.
Each mindful breath, each gentle pause,
Nurtures courage and quiet cause.
Even in shadow, life prepares,
For warmth, for blooms, and tender cares.
Step softly into this early light,
Let patience guide your day and night.
Though chill remains and clouds may stay,
Your inner strength will light your way.
Trust the garden, tender and true,
It blooms with hope, calm, and you.

Affirmation: Your heart awakens with patience, hope, and quiet strength.

15th April
The Emerging Green

Notice the tender green unfurling on branches once bare, each leaf a quiet miracle of patience and return. Their soft brightness whispers of resilience, reminding you that growth is often slow, yet steady, shaped by light and time. Today, let this new green guide your heart towards calm strength, showing that even after long stillness, renewal always comes. Each mindful breath, each gentle pause, is like sunlight caught on a leaf's surface, nourishing what is ready to awaken within you. Think of the blackbird once more, darting through hedgerows now touched with colour, its song carrying both memory and promise. As leaves reach for the sky with quiet certainty, so too does your spirit stretch toward what lies ahead—patient, strong, and filled with hope. Allow this gentle emergence to steady your day and remind you that you, too, are part of this unfolding rhythm of life.

Affirmation: Your heart grows quietly, nurtured by hope, patience, and strength.

16th April
The Flowing Brook

Listen to the brook as it threads its way over stone and soil, its voice soft yet unwavering, a song of persistence in motion. Even when its path is hidden beneath roots or shaded banks, the water finds its way, always moving forward. Today, let this quiet current remind you that your own life also flows steadily, carrying strength and hope even when unseen. Each mindful pause, each gentle act of care, is like a ripple spreading across the surface, shaping the journey in small but certain ways. Think of the hare pausing to drink at the water's edge, its stillness and alertness part of the same rhythm as the stream—it knows the value of both rest and movement. So too does your spirit: steady, resilient, and quietly alive with courage. Trust these subtle currents to guide you, for they hold within them the promise of calm and renewal.

Affirmation: You flow steadily with life, guided by hope, calm, and resilience.

17th April
The Morning Light

Notice the sun rising softly, spilling light across fields and gardens. Today, let it illuminate your mind and heart, bringing hope, calm, and courage. Each mindful breath and gentle movement nurtures your inner strength. Even in grey or tiring moments, trust that light persists within and around you. Allow this morning glow to fill your day with quiet optimism and renewal.

Affirmation: You welcome the light of hope, courage, and calm into your heart.

18th April
The Tender Meadow

Step into the meadow where early shoots rise through grass and soil, their tender green swaying gently in the April light. What begins as the smallest stirring soon spreads into a living carpet, proof that persistence often wears the face of quietness. Today, let this meadow remind you that your own resilience, though sometimes unseen, is steady and sure. Each breath, each pause, each mindful step is like a drop of rain nourishing the roots, helping growth along in its own patient time. Even in moments of stillness or uncertainty, life is unfurling within you, just as it does across the fields. Picture the swallow dipping low over the meadow, skimming the air with grace; it shows how movement and renewal weave together with ease. Like these tender shoots, your heart stretches towards its own season of bloom, carrying courage and calm within its unfolding.

Affirmation: You grow quietly, guided by hope, patience, and inner strength.

19th April
The Spring Awakening

A field awakens beneath soft skies,
Green shoots lifting where frost still lies.
Though winter lingers, cold and slow,
Life persists, and hope will grow.
Your spirit moves like this tender land,
Steady, patient, guided by your hand.
Each mindful breath, each gentle pause,
Nurtures courage and quiet cause.
Even in shadow, life prepares,
For blooms, for warmth, and open airs.
Step softly into this early light,
Let patience guide your day and night.
Though chill remains and clouds may stay,
Your inner calm shines bright today.
Trust the awakening, tender and true,
It blooms with hope, strength, and you.

Affirmation: Your heart awakens with calm, patience, and quiet courage.

20th April
The Gentle Rainfall

Notice the April rain as it falls with soft persistence, kissing leaf and earth alike, weaving silver threads across the day. Each drop carries quiet nourishment, seeping into soil, coaxing roots to deepen and blossoms to stir awake. Today, let this tender rhythm remind you that strength often builds in the gentlest of ways— through patience, through small continuities, through trust in what is unseen. Each mindful breath, each pause of stillness, is like the rain itself, feeding your inner ground with calm and courage. Even when skies feel heavy or the day wears long, life is quietly preparing its brightness beneath the surface. Picture the tree frog in distant forests, singing joyfully as the rains return, knowing the water brings renewal. So too does your spirit lift with this soft falling, steadying itself in hope, resilience, and quiet grace.

Affirmation: You are nourished by gentle moments, patience, and quiet courage.

21st April
The Awakening Tree

April leans softly upon the land, and the trees begin their quiet labour, swelling with tender buds that promise green abundance. Each small unfurling is a hymn to endurance, a reminder that life returns with patience and quiet resolve. As you walk beneath these awakening branches, imagine your own heart learning the same rhythm — steady, silent, and sure. Like a deer stepping gently through the morning mist, you too may move forward with grace, carrying both vulnerability and quiet strength. Even when weariness shadows you, know that growth is still at work within, unseen yet steadfast. Trust this season of renewal, and let its calmness steady your spirit. For in each mindful breath, hope takes root, and in each pause, courage quietly blooms.

Affirmation: You grow steadily, nurtured by hope, patience, and inner strength.

22nd April
The First Bees

April's light lingers tenderly on the blossoms, and from their fragile cups rises the hum of the first bees. Small though they are, their flight is steadfast, weaving promise into the morning air. Watch how they move with quiet diligence, each visit a testament to persistence and quiet faith in the turning seasons. So too may your spirit learn from their rhythm — gentle, patient, yet determined in its course. Even when difficulties press upon you, let your heart, like the bee, continue its work with unshaken resolve. Within the simplest acts of care and breath, renewal is already stirring, unseen yet certain. Trust that strength, born in silence, is gathering to carry you forward.

Affirmation: You persist gently, nurturing your spirit with hope, patience, and courage.

23rd April
The Soft Breeze

Feel the breeze dancing softly through branches and leaves, playful and light. Today, let it remind you that life moves gently, even when change is slow. Each breath, each pause, each mindful step strengthens your spirit and encourages resilience. Even in quiet or solitary moments, trust the subtle rhythm of life to carry you forward. Allow this gentle movement to bring calm and hope to your heart.

Affirmation: You move gently through life, guided by hope, calm, and patience.

24th April
The Spring Stream

A stream winds gently through the waking land,
Soft waters moving past stones and sand.
Though winter's chill may still remain,
Life flows onward through sun and rain.
Your spirit moves like this tender stream,
Quietly, patiently, following its dream.
Each mindful breath, each gentle pause,
Nurtures strength and quiet cause.
Even in shadow, life prepares,
For warmth, for growth, and open airs.
Step softly into this flowing light,
Let patience guide your day and night.
Though clouds may linger and winds may bite,
Your inner calm shines steady and bright.
Trust the stream, gentle and true,
It flows with hope, strength, and you.

Affirmation: Your heart flows with patience, hope, and quiet courage.

25th April
The Soft Earth

Beneath April's tender sun, the earth softens and warms, breathing quietly beneath your steps. Its patience is profound, holding within it the promise of blossoms yet to come, roots yet to deepen. As you pause upon this living ground, feel its steady strength lending calm to your own spirit. Like the lion who rests upon the grass before rising in quiet majesty, you too may find resilience in stillness. Even when uncertainty lingers, know that unseen growth is unfolding within, preparing to rise in its season. Each mindful breath is a seed of courage, each moment of pause a root of peace. Trust the earth's gentle wisdom, and let it carry you through the day with quiet hope.

Affirmation: You are grounded, resilient, and quietly growing with hope and calm.

26th April
The Morning Light

Morning arrives in April with a hush of gold, spilling softly across hedgerows, fields, and gardens. The light lingers tenderly, a quiet blessing upon all it touches, whispering of renewal and gentle strength. Let this radiance enter your heart, where it may kindle hope and steady courage. Like the swallow lifting effortlessly into the dawn sky, may you rise with quiet grace, carried by trust in what the day will bring. Even when shadows weigh upon you, know that light endures, glowing steadfast within. Each breath is a reminder of this inner flame, each pause a moment of calm strength. Walk with the morning, and let its glow guide your steps towards gentle renewal.

Affirmation: You welcome the light of hope, courage, and calm into your heart.

27th April
The Tender Meadow

April's meadows stir with fragile shoots, their green blades swaying gently beneath the breeze's quiet song. Each tender stem is a lesson in persistence, rising from the softened earth with steady faith in the sun. As you walk through this living carpet, let its quiet resilience mirror your own. Like a hare pausing watchfully among the grasses, you too may hold both stillness and strength within you. Even when challenges cloud the day, trust that your spirit, like the meadow, is quietly renewing itself, unseen yet steadfast. Each mindful breath plants hope, each pause waters patience, and each small act of care nourishes strength. Life moves forward gently, and so do you.

Affirmation: You grow quietly, guided by hope, patience, and inner strength.

28th April
The Awakening Fields

Fields awaken beneath soft skies,
Green shoots rising where frost still lies.
Though winter lingers with quiet chill,
Life persists, with hope and will.
Your heart moves like this tender land,
Steady, patient, guided by your hand.
Each mindful breath, each gentle pause,
Nurtures courage and quiet cause.
Even in shadow, life prepares,
For warmth, for growth, and tender cares.
Step softly into this gentle light,
Let patience guide you day and night.
Though chill remains and clouds may stay,
Your inner strength will light your way.
Trust the fields, tender and true,
They bloom with hope, courage, and you.

Affirmation: Your heart awakens with patience, hope, and quiet strength.

29th April
The Blossoming Air

April scatters petals into the breeze, and the air grows fragrant with promise. Blossoms drift like fleeting stars, their beauty brief yet radiant, reminding us to cherish the present. Stand beneath their delicate shower and feel the tender joy of impermanence. Like a butterfly rising on fragile wings, you too may find renewal in lightness and release. Even in moments of doubt, trust that beauty still lingers around you, soft as falling petals, certain as the turning of spring. Each mindful breath lifts the heart, each pause gathers calm, and each moment savoured plants seeds of quiet joy. Allow the blossoming air to carry you gently forward.

Affirmation: You move gently through life, nurtured by hope, calm, and courage.

30th April — Monthly Reflection Poem
April's Quiet Renewal

The earth awakens beneath soft skies,
Tender shoots lifting where frost still lies.
Your heart, like the soil, has rested and stirred,
Nurtured by patience, hope, and each word.
Each breath, each pause, each mindful act,
Carries courage, calm, and quiet impact.
Though chill may linger and clouds may stay,
Your inner strength persists every day.
Step softly into this gentle light,
Let renewal guide your heart tonight.
Through quiet moments and gentle days,
Hope blooms softly in tender ways.
Trust the rhythm, patient and true,
April carries calm, strength, and you.
Your spirit awakens, steady and strong,
Guided by hope and courage all month long.

Affirmation: You carry patience, hope, and quiet courage through every day.

MAY

1st May – Monthly Opening Poem

The Blooming Dawn

May arrives with gentle warmth,
Soft sunlight spreading through the earth.
Blossoms stretch beneath tender skies,
Their quiet beauty opens your eyes.
The world exhales a fragrant song,
Inviting your heart to grow strong.
Even amidst lingering shadows or chill,
Life awakens, patient and still.
Each mindful breath, each gentle pause,
Nurtures courage and hope because
Your spirit, like the flowers, blooms slow,
Steadily, softly, letting beauty show.
May whispers gently, patient and true,
"I hold renewal, strength, and hope for you."

Affirmation: You welcome renewal, hope, and gentle courage this May.

2nd May
The Whisper of Leaves

Hear the leaves rustling softly in the morning breeze, their light and purposeful dance accompanied by the darting flight of a swallow, and let this gentle cadence mirror your own steadfast progress through life's quiet journey. Each breath and mindful act weaves resilience, patience, and calm into your soul, a tranquil thread that holds firm even amidst the mists of uncertainty. Your spirit flows like leaves swaying on a tender wind, graceful and resolute, so allow the soft murmur of nature's embrace and the bird's swift grace to kindle your courage and hope, illuminating your day with a gentle, steadfast glow.

Affirmation: You move gently with life, guided by hope, calm, and patience.

3rd May
The Warm Sunlight

Feel the warmth of the sun caressing your skin, a tender yet radiant blessing, and let this gentle heat infuse your heart with hope, courage, and a profound calm that steadies your spirit. Each mindful pause and deliberate act becomes a sacred offering, nurturing an inner strength that thrives even when grey clouds linger or moments drag slowly by. Trust that your spirit grows with the quiet persistence of buds preparing to burst forth, and let the sunlight's embrace remind you that consistent, tender care cultivates resilience and renewal, a light that never fades.

Affirmation: You are warmed by hope, courage, and the steady light of renewal.

4th May
The Flowing Stream

Observe a stream meandering through soft grass, its gentle yet persistent flow mirrored by the graceful glide of an otter along its banks, and let this steady movement reflect the subtle continuity within your own existence amidst the rustling reeds. Each mindful breath and quiet pause nurtures strength and hope, a serene current that carries you forward even through the shadows of uncertainty or the weight of fatigue. Your spirit moves with graceful determination, shaping courage and renewal, so trust the stream's rhythmic pulse to guide your heart gently, offering peace and purpose throughout your day as nature whispers its timeless song through the flowing waters.

Affirmation: Your spirit flows steadily, nurtured by calm, hope, and resilience.

5th May
The First Bees

Watch bees flitting among early blooms, their diligent and diminutive forms imbued with purposeful grace as a ladybird ascends a leaf with delicate precision nearby, and let their quiet persistence inspire a resilience that resonates within your soul. Each mindful act and breath nurtures courage, hope, and a tranquil calm, a gentle labour that thrives even amidst life's trials. Your heart works silently, preparing for renewal with the tender care of bees tending blossoms, so allow this rhythm to shape patience and strength, a harmonious force that blooms within you with each passing, sacred moment as the flowers nod in approval.

Affirmation: You persist gently, nurtured by hope, patience, and courage.

6th May
The Gentle Breeze

Feel the breeze brushing softly through the trees, a tender and playful zephyr where a hare bounds with joyful abandon, and let it remind you that life moves with a steady grace, even when the pace of change feels languid and unseen. Each breath and mindful pause strengthens your spirit, kindling a quiet courage that endures through still or solitary moments. Trust the subtle rhythm of this gentle wind, and allow its ethereal touch to fill your heart with calm, hope, and patience, a soothing balm that guides your journey forward as the fields sway gently and the air dances with life.

Affirmation: You move gently through life, guided by hope, calm, and resilience.

7th May
Whispers of Renewal

The morning breaks with a tender glow,
Soft winds stir where the blossoms grow.
Streams run steady, their voices clear,
Carrying whispers that calm the ear.
A fox moves lightly through fields of green,
Silent strength in the spaces unseen.
Petals drift, and the heart takes flight,
Like a butterfly rising in gentle light.
The meadow bends to the breath of spring,
Holding the promise each season will bring.
Roots grow quietly beneath the ground,
Strength in silence, steady and sound.
The sky unfolds in a cloak of blue,
A gentle reminder of all that is true.
Each pause a moment to rest and be,
Opening the heart to serenity.
Walk with the day in calm embrace,
Trust in the rhythm of time and space.

Affirmation: You move gently with the rhythm of the day, rooted in strength and open to renewal.

8th May
The Blooming Tree

Behold a tree bursting into blossoms, each flower a testament to gentle persistence unfurling with quiet elegance as a squirrel leaps with nimble grace among its branches, and let this serene growth mirror the resilience blossoming within your own heart. Each mindful breath and deliberate pause nurtures hope, courage, and a tranquil calm, a nurturing force that thrives even amidst fatigue or doubt. Your spirit grows steadily, reaching toward renewal like the tree stretching toward the sun, and allow this graceful expansion to fill your soul with patience and a quiet, enduring strength that lights your path as the canopy whispers above.

Affirmation: You grow steadily, nurtured by hope, patience, and gentle courage.

9th May
The Rising Sun

Feel the soft warmth of morning sunlight spilling across fields and gardens, a golden tide of renewal where a deer grazes with serene dignity, and let its tender glow fill your heart with hope, calm, and a rejuvenating spirit. Each breath and mindful pause nurtures resilience and inner strength, a quiet power that rises even through the grey haze of challenging hours. Trust that your spirit carries courage and patience with graceful poise, and allow this gentle illumination to guide your thoughts and actions, weaving a path of serenity through your day as the landscape glows with life's promise.

Affirmation: You are warmed by hope, courage, and the steady light of renewal.

10th May
The Soft Rain

Hear gentle rain tapping leaves and earth, a soothing and persistent lullaby accompanied by the resonant croak of a frog in the distance, and let each delicate drop remind you that quiet, steady nourishment fosters growth and healing within your soul. Each mindful breath and small pause nurtures strength, patience, and a tranquil calm, a restorative balm that endures even through difficult or tiring moments. Your heart continues to grow and renew with resilient grace, so allow the rhythm of the rain to restore your spirit, inspiring hope with every tender note as the earth drinks deeply and the pond ripples.

Affirmation: You are nurtured by gentle moments, patience, and quiet strength.

11th May
The First Butterflies

Notice the delicate flutter of butterflies among early blossoms, their light and graceful dance echoed by the gentle hum of a bumblebee, and let their movement inspire a resilience that stirs within your heart. Each mindful act and gentle pause nurtures hope and calm, a serene energy that flows steadily even amidst uncertainty. Your spirit moves with patient grace, carrying renewal like butterflies dancing in sunlight, so allow your heart to open slowly to joy and growth, a tender blossoming under nature's watchful gaze as the air hums with life.

Affirmation: You move gracefully through life, guided by hope, calm, and patience.

12th May
The Flowing Brook

Listen to a brook flowing over stones, its steady and persistent murmur a hymn of life where a water vole skims the surface with silent grace, and let its gentle movement remind you that existence continues quietly, even when progress feels elusive. Each mindful pause and breath nurtures your spirit with resilience and calm, a quiet strength that holds firm through still or challenging moments. Trust that your heart is quietly shaping hope and renewal, and allow the flowing water to guide your day with gentle patience, a soothing rhythm for your soul amidst the rippling brook and the vole's gentle splash.

Affirmation: Your spirit flows steadily, nurtured by calm, hope, and quiet strength.

13th May
The Gentle Breeze

Feel the breeze rustling through leaves and flowers, a soft and tender whisper where a blackbird sings with mellifluous charm, and let it remind you that life moves with gentle elegance, even when change remains unseen or slow. Each mindful breath and pause nurtures courage, calm, and hope, a quiet vitality that grows steadily within your heart. Even in moments of solitude, trust this gentle wind to prepare you for renewal, and allow its ethereal caress to fill your spirit with patience and a serene, enduring strength as the blossoms sway and the blackbird's song fills the air.

Affirmation: You move gently through life, nurtured by hope, calm, and resilience.

14th May
The Awakening Garden

A garden wakes beneath soft skies,
Tender buds lifting where frost still lies.
Though morning opens with quiet chill,
Life persists, with hope and will.
Your spirit moves like this gentle land,
Steady, patient, guided by your hand.
Each mindful breath, each gentle pause,
Nurtures courage and quiet cause.
Even in shadow, life prepares,
For warmth, for growth, and tender cares.
Step softly into this early light,
Let patience guide your day and night.
Though clouds remain and winds may bite,
Your inner strength shines calm and bright.
Trust the garden, tender and true,
It blooms with hope, courage, and you.

Affirmation: Your heart awakens with calm, hope, and quiet strength.

15th May
The Soft Earth

Notice the earth beneath your feet, warming beneath gentle sunlight with a nurturing embrace as worms toil with silent dedication below, and let this grounding presence remind you of your own quiet resilience, a steadfast foundation within. Each mindful breath and deliberate pause nurtures courage, hope, and patience, a tender cultivation that thrives even in still or uncertain moments. Trust that your spirit grows steadily, and like fertile soil preparing for blooms, your heart readies itself for renewal and strength, a quiet promise beneath your every step as the soil breathes life and the worms weave their quiet work.

Affirmation: You are grounded, resilient, and quietly growing with patience and hope.

16th May
The Singing Birds

Listen to birds greeting the morning with songs soft yet persistent, a melodic ode to life where a thrush joins with its resonant trill, and let their melodies inspire your own quiet courage, a gentle flame within. Each mindful breath and pause nurtures hope, calm, and resilience, a harmonious strength that endures amidst challenges. Your spirit moves steadily, carrying patience and quiet power, so allow the songs of nature to fill your heart with gentle optimism and renewal, a symphony to guide your day as the air fills with their song and the trees stand witness.

Affirmation: Your spirit sings quietly, guided by hope, patience, and calm.

17th May
The First Blossoms

Notice flowers opening their petals to the sunlight, tender and determined in their quiet beauty as a butterfly alights with delicate poise nearby, and let their persistence remind you of your own steady growth, a graceful ascent. Each mindful breath and gentle pause nurtures courage, hope, and calm, a serene force that blossoms even amidst uncertainty or fatigue. Your spirit unfurls quietly, preparing for renewal, and like petals opening in spring, your heart expands with patience and gentle strength, a radiant bloom within as the garden thrives and the butterfly dances.

Affirmation: You bloom quietly, nurtured by hope, patience, and inner courage.

18th May
The Flowing Stream

Notice a stream winding through green meadows, soft yet persistent in its tranquil journey as a kingfisher flashes with iridescent splendour overhead, and let its gentle rhythm remind you that life continues, even when change unfolds slowly. Each mindful act and quiet pause nurtures resilience, patience, and calm, a steady current that flows through moments of challenge. Your spirit moves with quiet determination, carrying hope and courage, so allow the stream's flow to guide your heart gently, a soothing melody for your soul amidst the rippling waters and the kingfisher's swift dive.

Affirmation: Your spirit flows steadily, guided by hope, calm, and quiet strength.

19th May
The Spring Renewal

Rivers swell with the softest rain,
Carving paths through earth's domain.
Though storms may linger, clouds still weep,
The waters rise from winter's sleep.
Your spirit flows as streams unbind,
Clear and gentle, yet strong in mind.
Each moment's breath, each quiet flow,
Carries strength the heart will know.
Even in shadow, currents gleam,
Bearing whispers, hope, and dream.
Step lightly where the waters run,
Their song begins, the day is won.
Though tides may shift and eddies sway,
Your inner calm holds steady each day.
Trust renewal, fluid and bright,
It guides you onward, pure in light.

Affirmation: Your spirit flows with calm resilience, hope, and quiet strength.

20th May
The Gentle Breeze

Feel the breeze brushing softly through tall grass and budding flowers, a delicate whisper where a rabbit hops with gentle curiosity, and let its quiet movement remind you that existence flows gently, even when change seems to linger. Each mindful breath and pause nurtures calm, patience, and hope, a tender strength that endures through uncertainty or fatigue. Trust that your spirit moves steadily, carrying quiet power, and allow this gentle wind to fill your heart with courage and renewal, a soft breeze to guide your soul as the landscape sways and the rabbit pauses to listen.

Affirmation: You move gently through life, nurtured by hope, patience, and resilience.

21st May
The Warm Sunlight

Notice the sun spreading warmth across fields and trees, tender and bright in its golden embrace as a pheasant struts with regal poise nearby, and let this soft light fill your heart with calm, courage, and hope, a radiant blessing. Each mindful breath and pause nurtures resilience and quiet strength, a steady glow that persists through grey or tiring moments. Trust that your spirit grows with graceful determination, and allow the gentle sun to guide your thoughts and actions, illuminating your path with patience and renewal as the earth basks in its glow and the pheasant calls.

Affirmation: You are warmed by hope, courage, and the steady light of renewal.

22nd May
The Flowing Stream

Watch a stream gliding over stones and earth, persistent yet gentle in its serene dance as a trout leaps with silvery grace, and let its steady flow remind you that life continues quietly, even in subtle ways. Each mindful breath and thoughtful pause nurtures resilience, patience, and hope, a tranquil force that moves through still or challenging moments. Your heart advances steadily toward growth and renewal, so allow the stream's rhythm to guide your spirit with gentle calm, a peaceful current for your day amidst the flowing waters and the trout's fleeting arc.

Affirmation: Your spirit flows steadi y, guided by hope, patience, and quiet strength.

23rd May
The First Butterflies

Notice the flutter of butterflies among early blooms, delicate yet determined in their airy grace as a dragonfly hovers with iridescent wings nearby, and let their gentle persistence inspire your own quiet courage and resilience. Each mindful act and pause nurtures hope, patience, and calm, a light strength that endures amidst challenges. Your spirit moves steadily, carrying renewal, and like butterflies dancing in the sun, your heart opens to gentle joy and growth, a tender blossom unfurling within as the air hums with life and the dragonfly glides.

Affirmation: You move gracefully, nurtured by hope, patience, and quiet courage.

24th May
The Awakening Garden

Walk through a garden where shoots and blossoms stretch toward the sun, a living tapestry of quiet growth as a robin flits with cheerful melody among the branches, and let their serene progress mirror your own steady advancement. Each mindful breath and gentle pause nurtures hope, courage, and calm, a nurturing force that thrives even amidst fatigue or doubt. Trust that your spirit prepares for renewal, and like tender blossoms reaching skyward, your heart expands with patience and gentle strength, a radiant promise within your soul as the garden thrives and the robin sings.

Affirmation: You grow quietly, guided by hope, patience, and inner strength.

25th May
The Spring Stream

A stream winds gently through the waking land,
Soft waters flowing over stones and sand.
Though winter's chill may linger near,
Life continues with courage clear.
Your heart moves like this gentle flow,
Steady, patient, letting hope grow.
Each mindful breath, each careful pause,
Nurtures resilience and quiet cause.
Even in shadow, life prepares,
For warmth, for growth, and tender cares.
Step softly into this morning light,
Let patience guide your day and night.
Though clouds may linger and winds may sway,
Your inner calm shines bright each day.
Trust the stream, gentle and true,
It flows with hope, strength, and you.

Affirmation: Your heart moves steadily with patience, hope, and quiet courage.

26th May
The Soft Earth

Notice the earth beneath your feet, warming beneath spring sunshine with a nurturing glow as moles tunnel with quiet diligence below, and let this grounding presence remind you of your own resilience, a quiet anchor within. Each mindful breath and gentle pause nurtures hope, calm, and patience, a tender cultivation that flourishes even in solitude or uncertainty. Like fertile soil supporting tender blooms, your heart prepares for growth and renewal, a steadfast promise beneath your every step as the earth pulses with life and the moles weave their unseen paths.

Affirmation: You are grounded, resilient, and quietly growing with hope and patience.

27th May
The Singing Birds

Listen to birds greeting the morning with songs soft yet persistent, a melodic tribute to life where a chaffinch adds its delicate trill, and let their melodies inspire your own quiet courage, a gentle spark within. Each mindful breath and pause nurtures hope, calm, and strength, a harmonious force that endures through challenges. Your spirit moves steadily, carrying patience and quiet power, so allow the songs of nature to fill your heart with gentle optimism and renewal, a symphony to guide your day as the air fills with their song and the trees stand as silent witnesses.

Affirmation: Your spirit sings quietly, guided by hope, patience, and calm.

28th May
The First Blossoms

Notice flowers opening their petals to gentle sunlight, delicate yet determined. Today, let their quiet growth remind you of your own steady resilience. Each mindful breath, each pause nurtures courage, patience, and calm. Even in moments of uncertainty or fatigue, your spirit blossoms quietly, preparing for renewal. Like petals unfurling in spring, your heart opens with gentle strength and hope.

Affirmation: You bloom patiently, nurtured by hope, patience, and inner courage.

29th May
The Flowing Brook

Watch a brook winding through green meadows, soft and persistent in its tranquil flow as a moorhen glides with serene elegance across, and let its gentle rhythm remind you that life continues steadily, even when progress feels elusive. Each mindful pause and deliberate breath nurtures resilience, patience, and calm, a quiet strength that moves through solitude or challenge. Your heart advances steadily toward growth and renewal, so allow the brook's flow to guide your spirit with gentle courage, a soothing balm for your day as the waters ripple and the moorhen drifts.

Affirmation: Your spirit flows steadily, guided by hope, calm, and quiet strength.

30th May
The Awakening Fields

Fields awaken beneath warming skies,
Tender shoots lift where frost still lies.
Though morning lingers with subtle chill,
Life returns with courage and will.
Your heart moves like this gentle land,
Steady, patient, guided by your hand.
Each mindful breath, each careful pause,
Nurtures hope and quiet cause.
Even in shadow, life prepares,
For warmth, for growth, and tender cares.
Step softly into this gentle light,
Let patience guide your day and night.
Though clouds may linger and winds may sway,
Your inner strength shines calm each day.
Trust the fields, tender and true,
They bloom with hope, patience, and you.

Affirmation: Your heart awakens with patience, hope, and quiet courage.

31st May — Monthly Reflection Poem
May's Gentle Renewal

The earth is bright beneath warming skies,
Soft blossoms open as spring and summer tries.
Your heart, like the soil, has rested and stirred,
Nurtured by patience, hope, and each word.
Each mindful breath, each gentle pause,
Strengthens courage, calm, and quiet cause.
Though clouds may linger and winds may bite,
Your inner strength shines steady and bright.
Step softly into this gentle light,
Let renewal guide your heart tonight.
Through quiet moments and tender days,
Hope blooms softly in patient ways.
Trust the rhythm, patient and true,
May carries calm strength, and you.
Your spirit awakens, resilient and strong,
Guided by hope and courage all month long.

Affirmation: You carry patience, hope, and quiet courage through every day.

JUNE

1st June – Monthly Opening Poem

The Sunlit Meadow

June arrives with longer days,
Soft sunlight spreading gentle rays.
Meadows awaken, bright and green,
A quiet beauty, tender and serene.
The world hums softly with life renewed,
Each leaf and blossom perfectly imbued.
Even when shadows linger near,
Your heart is strengthened, calm, and clear.
Step into this month with gentle grace,
Let warmth and hope fill every space.
June whispers softly, patient and true,
"I hold renewal, courage, and light for you."

Affirmation: You welcome warmth, growth, and gentle courage this June.

2nd June
The Flowing Stream

June unfolds with soft light, and the stream winds gracefully through meadows rich with summer's green. Its waters slip over stones and roots, carrying a quiet song of persistence and ease. Watch how it never hurries, yet always finds its way, reminding you that life moves forward even when its pace feels gentle or unseen. Like an otter gliding with playful ease along the current, your spirit too can learn to trust in the flow, finding strength in both stillness and motion. Each mindful breath anchors you in patience, each pause nourishes quiet resilience. Even when challenges weigh upon you, the current within your heart moves steadily towards growth and renewal. Let the stream's calm rhythm carry you, steady and sure, into the unfolding day.

Affirmation: Your spirit flows steadily, guided by hope, calm, and quiet strength.

3rd June
The First Bees

Notice bees visiting early blooms, their small yet determined forms a testament to nature's quiet resolve as a hedgehog snuffles gently through the undergrowth nearby, and let their diligent grace inspire your own gentle courage that stirs within. Each mindful act and thoughtful pause weaves hope, patience, and calm into the tapestry of your soul, a tender labour that thrives even amidst life's trials. Your spirit moves steadily, carrying strength and quiet resilience, a silent force preparing for renewal and growth, so allow the bees' harmonious dance and the hedgehog's soft presence to nurture your heart, a sanctuary of peace amidst the blooming fields.

Affirmation: You persist gently, nurtured by hope, patience, and inner courage.

4th June
The Gentle Breeze

Feel the breeze rustling softly through leaves and flowers, tender and playful. Today, let it remind you that life moves quietly, even when change feels slow or unseen. Each mindful breath, each gentle pause nurtures courage, calm, and hope. Even in still or solitary moments, trust that your spirit grows steadily. Allow this gentle wind to fill your heart with patience, renewal, and quiet strength.

Affirmation: You move gently through life, nurtured by hope, calm, and resilience.

5th June
The Blossoming Tree

Notice a tree lifting its buds and blossoms toward the sun, patient and strong as a squirrel leaps with nimble grace among its branches, and let this quiet growth mirror your own inner strength and steady courage that blossoms within. Each mindful breath and deliberate pause nurtures hope, calm, and resilience, a nurturing force that endures even amidst the shadows of fatigue or the mists of uncertainty. Your spirit grows slowly but surely, a testament to resilience, and like the tree reaching upward with timeless elegance, your heart opens gently to renewal and joy, a radiant promise carried on the summer breeze.

Affirmation: You grow steadily, nurtured by hope, patience, and gentle courage.

6th June
The Singing Birds

Listen to birds greeting the morning, their songs delicate yet persistent. Today, let their melodies inspire your own quiet courage and hope. Each mindful act and gentle pause nurtures resilience, patience, and calm. Even amidst challenges, your spirit moves steadily, carrying strength and renewal. Allow the songs of nature to fill your heart with gentle joy and confidence.

Affirmation: Your spirit sings quietly, guided by hope, patience, and calm.

7th June
The Summer Meadow

A meadow wakes beneath soft skies,
Green shoots rising where frost still lies.
Though winter's chill may linger near,
Life flows onward with courage clear.
Your heart moves like this gentle land,
Steady, patient, guided by your hand.
Each mindful breath, each gentle pause,
Nurtures hope and quiet cause.
Even in shadow, life prepares,
For warmth, for growth, and tender cares.
Step softly into this morning light,
Let patience guide your day and night.
Though clouds may linger and winds may sway,
Your inner calm shines bright each day.
Trust the meadow, tender and true,
It blooms with hope, courage, and you.

Affirmation: Your heart awakens with patience, hope, and quiet courage.

8th June
The Flowing Brook

Notice a brook winding through sunlit fields, gentle yet persistent as a kingfisher darts with iridescent splendour above, and let its soft rhythm remind you that life moves steadily, even when progress feels elusive amidst the summer's glow. Each mindful breath and quiet pause nurtures resilience, patience, and hope, a tranquil force that sustains your spirit through still or challenging moments. Your heart flows steadily toward growth and renewal, a silent journey mirrored by the brook's gentle dance, so allow its soothing movement to guide your soul through the day, a poetic flow beneath the canopy of trees.

Affirmation: Your spirit flows calmly, nurtured by hope, patience, and inner strength.

9th June
The First Butterflies

Watch butterflies flutter among blossoming flowers, delicate yet determined. Today, let their quiet grace inspire your own steady courage. Each mindful act and gentle pause nurtures hope, calm, and resilience. Even in moments of uncertainty or fatigue, your spirit moves gracefully, carrying patience and gentle strength. Like wings catching sunlight, your heart opens quietly to joy and renewal.

Affirmation: You move gracefully, guided by hope, patience, and quiet courage.

10th June
The Soft Earth

Feel the earth warming beneath your feet, rich and steady as moles toil with quiet dedication below, and let this grounding presence remind you of your own quiet resilience that anchors your soul. Each mindful breath and deliberate pause nurtures hope, calm, and strength, a nurturing force that flourishes even in the stillness of uncertainty or the hush of solitary moments. Your spirit grows slowly but surely, a testament to endurance, and like fertile soil supporting the season's blooms, your heart prepares for growth, healing, and renewal, a sacred bond with the earth's summer pulse.

Affirmation: You are grounded, patient, and nurtured by hope and calm.

11th June
The Warm Sunlight

Notice sunlight spilling across leaves, blossoms, and meadows, tender yet bright. Today, let this soft glow fill your heart with hope, calm, and quiet courage. Each mindful breath and gentle pause nurtures resilience and patience. Even amidst fatigue or grey skies, trust that your spirit rises steadily, like petals reaching toward the sun. Allow the gentle illumination to guide your thoughts and actions with care and warmth.

Affirmation: You are warmed by hope, calm, and the steady light of renewal.

12th June
The Singing Birds

Hear birds welcoming the morning with soft yet persistent songs, their melodies joined by the delicate trill of a chaffinch, and let their ethereal voices inspire your own courage and hope that swell within your breast. Each mindful breath and pause nurtures patience, calm, and resilience, a harmonious force that flows steadily even amidst life's trials. Your spirit moves with gentle strength and renewal, a quiet power sustained by nature's chorus, so allow the songs of the dawn to fill your heart with peace, optimism, and quiet joy, a symphony echoing through the summer air.

Affirmation: Your spirit sings gently, guided by hope, patience, and calm.

13th June
The Gentle Breeze

Feel the breeze brushing softly across fields, trees, and flowers. Today, let it remind you that life flows gently, even when change is slow or unseen. Each mindful breath and thoughtful pause nurtures hope, patience, and calm. Even in quiet or solitary moments, your spirit grows steadily. Allow this gentle wind to fill your heart with courage, renewal, and quiet strength.

Affirmation: You move gently through life, nurtured by hope, patience, and resilience.

14th June
The Summer Stream

A stream winds gently through the sunlit land,
Soft waters flowing over stones and sand.
Though morning's chill may linger near,
Life continues with courage clear.
Your heart moves like this gentle flow,
Steady, patient, letting hope grow.
Each mindful breath, each careful pause,
Nurtures resilience and quiet cause.
Even in shadow, life prepares,
For warmth, for growth, and tender cares.
Step softly into this morning light,
Let patience guide your day and night.
Though clouds may linger and winds may sway,
Your inner calm shines bright each day.
Trust the stream, gentle and true,
It flows with hope, strength, and you.

Affirmation: Your heart awakens with patience, hope, and quiet courage.

15th June
The Awakening Garden

Walk through a garden where blooms reach toward the sun, their petals aglow as a robin flits with cheerful song among the branches, and let their gentle growth mirror your own quiet resilience that stirs within. Each mindful breath and pause nurtures hope, calm, and courage, a tender force that thrives even amidst the shadows of fatigue or the mists of uncertainty. Trust that your spirit prepares for renewal, a silent promise woven into your soul, and like tender petals stretching upward, your heart opens slowly, embracing gentle strength and quiet joy as the garden hums with summer's life.

Affirmation: You grow steadily, nurtured by hope, patience, and inner strength.

16th June
The Blossoming Tree

Notice a tree lifting its buds and blossoms to the light, patient and persistent. Today, let this quiet unfolding inspire your own steady courage. Each mindful act, each deliberate pause nurtures hope, patience, and calm. Even in moments of uncertainty, your spirit blooms slowly but surely. Like the tree reaching skyward, your heart opens gently to renewal and strength.

Affirmation: You bloom patiently, nurtured by hope, patience, and quiet courage.

17th June
The Flowing Brook

Watch a brook winding through lush meadows, gentle yet unceasing as a moorhen glides with serene elegance across its surface, and let its soft rhythm remind you that life moves steadily, even when progress seems a distant whisper. Each mindful breath and careful pause nurtures resilience, patience, and hope, a tranquil current that sustains your spirit through quiet or challenging moments. Your heart flows steadily toward growth and renewal, a graceful journey mirrored by the brook's dance, so allow its gentle movement to guide your soul with calm and courage as the summer waters sing.

Affirmation: Your spirit flows steadily, guided by hope, patience, and quiet strength.

18th June
The First Butterflies

Notice butterflies dancing among blooming flowers, delicate yet determined. Today, let their quiet grace inspire your own gentle courage. Each mindful act and thoughtful pause nurtures hope, calm, and resilience. Even amidst challenges, your spirit moves steadily, carrying patience and quiet strength. Like wings catching sunlight, your heart opens slowly to joy and gentle renewal.

Affirmation: You move gracefully, guided by hope, patience, and quiet courage.

19th June
The Summer Fields

Fields awaken beneath warming skies,
Tender shoots lift where frost still lies.
Though winter lingers with subtle chill,
Life continues with courage and will.
Your heart moves like this gentle land,
Steady, patient, guided by your hand.
Each mindful breath, each gentle pause,
Nurtures hope and quiet cause.
Even in shadow, life prepares,
For warmth, for growth, and tender cares.
Step softly into this morning light,
Let patience guide your day and night.
Though clouds may linger and winds may sway,
Your inner calm shines bright each day.
Trust the fields, tender and true,
They bloom with hope, patience, and you.

Affirmation: Your heart awakens with patience, hope, and quiet courage.

20th June
The Soft Earth

Feel the earth beneath your feet, rich and warm beneath the sun's tender gaze as moles toil with quiet dedication below, and let its steady presence remind you of your own quiet resilience that anchors your soul. Each mindful breath and gentle pause nurtures hope, patience, and calm, a nurturing force that flourishes even in the stillness of uncertainty or the hush of solitary moments. Your spirit grows steadily, a testament to endurance, and like fertile soil supporting the season's blossoms, your heart prepares for growth and renewal, a sacred bond with the earth's summer pulse as life stirs beneath.

Affirmation: You are grounded, patient, and nurtured by hope and calm.

21st June
The Singing Birds

Listen to the birds calling softly through the morning light, persistent and joyful. Today, let their melodies inspire your own quiet courage and optimism. Each mindful breath and gentle pause nurtures hope, patience, and resilience. Even amidst challenges, your spirit moves steadily, carrying gentle strength and renewal. Allow the songs of nature to fill your heart with calm and quiet joy.

Affirmation: Your spirit sings gently, guided by hope, patience, and calm.

22nd June
The Gentle Breeze

Notice a soft breeze moving through leaves and flowers, tender and persistent as a rabbit pauses with gentle curiosity, and let it remind you that life flows gently, even when change is slow or veiled in mystery. Each mindful breath and thoughtful pause nurtures patience, calm, and hope, a serene vitality that grows steadily within your spirit even in quiet or solitary moments. Trust this gentle wind to cradle your soul, and allow its ethereal touch to fill your heart with courage, renewal, and quiet strength, a poetic breath dancing through the summer's verdant expanse as the rabbit listens.

Affirmation: You move gently through life, nurtured by hope, patience, and resilience.

23rd June
The Blossoming Tree

Observe a tree lifting buds and blossoms toward the sunlight, patient and strong. Today, let its steady growth mirror your own quiet courage. Each mindful act, each deliberate pause nurtures hope, patience, and calm. Even in moments of fatigue or uncertainty, your spirit blooms slowly but surely. Like the tree reaching upward, your heart opens gently to renewal and inner strength.

Affirmation: You bloom patiently, nurtured by hope, patience, and quiet courage.

24th June
The Flowing Brook

Watch a brook winding through sunlit meadows, steady and gentle as a moorhen glides with serene elegance across its surface, and let its soft rhythm remind you that life moves forward, even when progress feels a distant whisper. Each mindful breath and careful pause nurtures resilience, patience, and hope, a tranquil current that sustains your spirit through quiet or challenging moments. Your heart flows steadily toward growth and renewal, a graceful journey mirrored by the brook's dance, so allow its gentle movement to guide your soul with calm and courage as the summer waters sing.

Affirmation: Your spirit flows steadily, guided by hope, patience, and quiet strength.

25th June
The Summer Meadow

A meadow wakes beneath the warming skies,
Green shoots rising where dew lies.
Though season's changes may remind of fear,
Life continues with courage clear.
Your heart moves like this gentle land,
Steady, patient, guided by your hand.
Each mindful breath, each gentle pause,
Nurtures hope and quiet cause.
Even in shadow, life prepares,
For warmth, for growth, and tender cares.
Step softly into this morning light,
Let patience guide your day and night.
Though clouds may linger and winds may sway,
Your inner calm shines bright each day.
Trust the meadow, tender and true,
It blooms with hope, patience, and you.

Affirmation: Your heart awakens with patience, hope, and quiet courage.

26th June
The Rising Sun

Notice the sun spilling golden light across fields and trees, warm and tender as a pheasant struts with regal poise through the undergrowth, and let its glow fill your heart with hope, calm, and quiet strength. Each mindful breath and gentle pause nurtures patience, resilience, and courage, a radiant force that rises steadily even amidst the mists of uncertainty or the weight of fatigue. Your spirit ascends like petals reaching toward the sun's embrace, and allow this soft illumination to guide your thoughts and actions with care and renewal, a beacon through the summer's golden haze as the fields shimmer.

Affirmation: You are warmed by hope, calm, and the steady light of renewal.

27th June
The First Butterflies

See butterflies flutter among early blooms, delicate yet persistent. Today, let their quiet grace inspire your own gentle courage. Each mindful act and deliberate pause nurtures hope, calm, and resilience. Even in challenging moments, your spirit moves gracefully, carrying patience and quiet strength. Like wings catching sunlight, your heart opens slowly to joy and renewal.

Affirmation: You move gracefully, guided by hope, patience, and quiet courage.

28th June
The Awakening Garden

Walk through a garden where blossoms stretch toward the sun, their petals aglow as a robin flits with cheerful song among the branches. Let their quiet growth mirror your own inner strength and resilience that blossoms within. Each mindful breath and gentle pause nurtures hope and patience, nurturing force that thrives even amidst the veils of uncertainty or the weight of fatigue. Trust that your spirit prepares for renewal, a silent promise woven into your soul, and like petals unfurling toward the light, your heart opens slowly to gentle strength and quiet joy as the garden hums with summer's life.

Affirmation: You grow steadily, nurtured by hope, patience, and inner strength.

29th June
The Flowing Stream

Notice a stream gliding over stones and through meadows, soft yet persistent. Today, let its gentle rhythm remind you that life moves steadily, even when progress seems slow. Each mindful breath and careful pause nurtures resilience, patience, and hope, a tranquil current that sustains your spirit through still or challenging moments. Your heart flows quietly toward growth and renewal, a graceful journey mirrored by the stream's dance, so allow its gentle current to guide your soul with calm and courage as the summer waters sing.

Affirmation: Your spirit flows steadily, guided by hope, patience, and quiet strength.

30th June — Monthly Reflection Poem
June's Radiant Renewal

The earth is bright beneath warming skies,
Soft blossoms opening as winter dies.
Your heart, like the soil, has rested and stirred,
Nurtured by patience, hope, and each word.
Each mindful breath, each gentle pause,
Strengthens courage, calm, and quiet cause.
Though clouds may linger and winds may bite,
Your inner strength shines steady and bright.
Step softly into this golden light,
Let renewal guide your heart tonight.
Through quiet moments and tender days,
Hope blooms softly in patient ways.
Trust the rhythm, patient and true,
June carries calm, courage, and you.
Your spirit awakens, resilient and strong,
Guided by hope and courage all month long.

Affirmation: You carry patience, hope, and quiet courage through every day.

JULY

1st July – Monthly Opening Poem

Whispers of the Meadow

July arrives with long, warm days,
Meadows glowing in golden rays.
The breeze stirs leaves and whispers low,
Emotions rise like tides that flow.
Some feelings gentle, soft, or bright,
Some restless, shadowed, or full of fright.
The sun reflects your inner light,
Even when your heart feels tight.
Observe each feeling without disdain,
Let joy and sorrow both remain.
Step into this month with mindful grace,
Feel each emotion, let calm embrace.
July reminds you, steady and true,
"I hold hope, courage, and peace for you."

Affirmation: You acknowledge your emotions and meet each day with gentle courage and mindful awareness.

2nd July
The Flowing Brook

Observe a brook winding through sunlit meadows, soft and persistent. Let it remind you that your emotions, like water, flow naturally — sometimes calm, sometimes swift, sometimes reflective. Each breath, each pause, nurtures patience, understanding, and gentle courage. Even when feelings feel overwhelming, your spirit can move steadily like water, observing without judgement. Let the brook carry your attention to the present, noticing the sparkle of sunlight and the murmurs of life.

Affirmation: Your emotions flow naturally, and you hold them with patience, calm, and acceptance.

3rd July
The Bees Among Flowers

Notice bees visiting early blooms, their diligent yet delicate forms a ballet of summer's purpose as a ladybird climbs a stem with quiet determination nearby, and let their persistence mirror your own capacity to notice and honour your emotions with graceful reverence. Each mindful act, each gentle pause, nurtures understanding, resilience, and calm, a tender cultivation that thrives even when emotions feel confusing or intense, like the hum of wings amid the petals. Even when feelings seem intricate or fervent, your heart can observe them, acknowledge them, and let them be, a serene acceptance guided by the warmth of the sun and the stillness of the earth that cradles all. Like the bees tending blossoms with unwavering care, your spirit tends each feeling with patience and poise, a harmonious dance woven into the fabric of summer's blooming tapestry, where the air shimmers with life.

Affirmation: You tend to your emotions with gentle care, allowing them to be and guiding them with calm awareness.

4th July
The Gentle Breeze

Feel the breeze moving softly through summer leaves, tender and persistent. Today, let it remind you that your feelings shift like the wind — some light, some heavy, some fleeting. Each breath nurtures patience and gentle acceptance. Even when emotions rise unexpectedly, your heart can receive them without judgement, observing the ebb and flow with steady grace. Let the wind carry your thoughts to the present moment, grounding you in nature's rhythm and your own inner calm.

Affirmation: You allow your feelings to shift and flow, meeting them with mindful calm and gentle acceptance.

5th July
The Blossoming Tree

Notice a tree lifting buds and blossoms toward the sunlight, patient and strong as a squirrel leaps with nimble elegance among its branches, and allow your heart to do the same—opening gently to each emotion, whether fleeting as a summer shower or deep as the roots below. Each mindful pause nurtures resilience, understanding, and calm, a tender force that endures even when feelings feel heavy or uncertain, like the weight of leaves in the breeze. Even when emotions seem intricate or profound, your spirit can bloom slowly, mirroring the tree's quiet strength that stands resolute through the seasons. Watch your emotions as you would leaves in sunlight—present, alive, and ever-changing, a poetic dance of light and shadow in the summer canopy.

Affirmation: You hold your feelings with patience and gentleness, letting them grow and unfold naturally.

6th July
The Flowing Stream

See a stream gliding over stones, soft yet persistent. Today, let its gentle rhythm remind you that your emotions move naturally — sometimes calm, sometimes turbulent, always part of life's flow. Each mindful breath nurtures patience, courage, and understanding. Even when feelings rise like sudden currents, your heart can observe without resistance, letting them pass while remaining grounded in the present. Allow the stream to guide your attention to the gentle movement of life around you.

Affirmation: Your emotions flow naturally, and you observe them with calm, patience, and mindful awareness.

7th July
The Summer Stream of Feeling

A stream winds gently through sunlit fields,
Soft waters reflecting what life yields.
Joy and sorrow, light and shadow too,
Each emotion a colour, a shade, a hue.
Your heart moves like this flowing stream,
Steady, patient, guided by dream.
Each mindful breath, each careful pause,
Nurtures hope, courage, and quiet cause.
Even when shadows linger near,
Your feelings are welcomed without fear.
Step softly into this summer light,
Let patience guide your day and night.
Though winds may stir and clouds may drift,
Your inner calm receives each gift.
Trust the stream of emotions, gentle and true,
It carries hope, courage, and you.

Affirmation: You meet all feelings with patience, courage, and gentle understanding.

8th July
The Morning Dew

Notice the dew sparkling on grass and leaves, fragile yet luminous as a spider weaves its silken web nearby, and allow each feeling—anticipation, weariness, joy, or worry—to shine gently in your awareness, a delicate glimmer in the summer dawn. Each mindful breath nourishes patience, calm, and quiet courage, a serene force that holds even when emotions feel fragile or overwhelming, like droplets quivering on a petal. Even when feelings seem ephemeral or intense, your heart can hold them with gentleness, letting them glimmer like dew in the morning sun's tender embrace. Observe your inner landscape with curiosity, tenderly welcoming what arises, a poetic reflection of the world's quiet beauty and the spider's intricate artistry.

Affirmation: You meet each feeling with gentle awareness and allow hope to shine through.

9th July
The Rustling Leaves

Hear leaves moving in the summer breeze, whispering softly. Today, let each rustle remind you that emotions shift and change, each one important and acknowledged. Each mindful pause nurtures resilience, calm, and understanding. Even when feelings stir uneasily, your heart can remain steady, observing and embracing each sensation with compassion. Allow nature's quiet rhythms to mirror your own inner tides.

Affirmation: You observe your emotions with kindness and trust in the gentle rhythm of life.

10th July
The Sun on the Pond

See sunlight dancing on water, bright and shimmering as a frog leaps with sudden grace from a lily pad, and let each reflection mirror the emotions within you—joy, fear, or quiet contemplation—a poetic play of light on the summer pond. Each mindful breath nurtures patience and hope, a serene anchor that holds even when feelings ripple unpredictably, like waves stirred by the frog's plunge. Even when emotions undulate with intensity, your heart can acknowledge them, holding them tenderly without judgement, a quiet acceptance reflected in the pond's tranquil depths. Like the pond mirroring the sky's vast expanse, you can reflect on your emotions with gentle grace, allowing the summer sun to illuminate your inner world.

Affirmation: You acknowledge your emotions and let hope guide your heart.

11th July
The Summer Meadow

Walk through a meadow alive with wildflowers and the hum of bees. Today, let each colour and movement remind you that emotions, too, are alive — diverse, shifting, and full of life. Each breath and gentle pause nurtures courage, calm, and understanding. Even when feelings feel intense, your spirit can hold them tenderly, like flowers in the sun. Allow nature's vitality to mirror your own inner strength.

Affirmation: You hold your emotions with courage and allow hope to bloom.

12th July
The Whispering Breeze

Feel a soft summer breeze across your face, gentle and persistent as a swallow soars with effortless elegance overhead, and notice how emotions, like the wind, can be subtle or strong, shifting and moving naturally through the air. Each mindful pause nurtures resilience, calm, and acceptance, a serene embrace that holds even when feelings feel restless or heavy, like gusts stirring the leaves. Even when emotions undulate with unrest, your heart can hold them with tenderness, letting them pass while remaining grounded in the present, a quiet poise amid the summer's vitality. Allow the wind's quiet guidance to bring clarity, peace, and hope, a poetic breath that dances through the landscape as the swallow glides.

Affirmation: You let your feelings move naturally, embracing them with calm and patience.

13th July
The Fluttering Butterfly

Watch a butterfly drift from bloom to bloom, delicate and free. Today, let its effortless movement remind you that emotions, too, can come and go. Each mindful breath nurtures calm, hope, and gentle acceptance. Even when feelings feel fleeting or overwhelming, your heart can acknowledge them, letting them rise and fall naturally. Like the butterfly in sunlight, your spirit moves with grace and resilience.

Affirmation: You allow your emotions to flow freely, embracing each one with gentle understanding.

14th July
The Summer River

A river winds beneath the golden skies,
Carrying laughter, sorrow, tears, and sighs.
Its waters shimmer in the morning light,
Reflecting each emotion, tender and bright.
Your heart moves like this flowing stream,
Steady, patient, nurturing each dream.
Each mindful breath, each gentle pause,
Strengthens calm, hope, and quiet cause.
Even when shadows linger near,
Your feelings are welcomed without fear.
Step softly into this summer day,
Let patience guide you along the way.
Though storms may stir and winds may blow,
Your inner strength continues to grow.
Trust the river, gentle and true,
It carries hope, courage, and you.

Affirmation: You meet all emotions with courage, hope, and gentle acceptance.

15th July
The Golden Fields

Notice fields glowing in the summer sun, warm and steady. Today, allow each feeling — calm or restless — to be acknowledged with gentle curiosity. Each mindful pause nurtures patience, resilience, and hope. Even when emotions rise unexpectedly, your heart can hold them without judgement, like the earth holds the roots of flourishing plants. Let the warmth of the sun remind you that hope persists within you.

Affirmation: You embrace your emotions with patience and allow hope to guide your spirit.

16th July
The Singing Birds

Hear birds greeting the morning with persistent song, their melodies joined by the resonant call of a cuckoo in the distance, and let their music remind you that every emotion, joyful or sorrowful, has a voice and a place in the symphony of your soul. Each mindful breath nurtures calm, courage, and understanding, a harmonious strength that endures even in moments of uncertainty, like the bird's unwavering tune. Even when feelings ripple with intensity, your heart can listen, honouring each one and allowing it to pass naturally, a serene acceptance reflected in the summer air. Like the birdsong filling the dawn, your spirit can hold space for all that arises, a poetic harmony woven into the fabric of life's abundance.

Affirmation: You listen to your feelings with compassion, allowing hope to rise in your heart.

17th July
The Blossoming Garden

Walk among blooms, petals reaching for the light as a butterfly alights with delicate poise on a flower, and allow your emotions to be like flowers—diverse, vibrant, and growing at their own pace in the summer's embrace. Each mindful breath nurtures acceptance, calm, and hope, a tender force that flourishes even when feelings feel heavy or complex, like the weight of dew on petals. Even when emotions undulate with depth, your heart can hold them tenderly, a serene poise amid the garden's vitality. Like a garden unfolding under the sun's golden rays, your inner world can flourish with patience and gentle awareness, a radiant tapestry of summer's beauty.

Affirmation: You allow your emotions to bloom, holding them with kindness and hope.

18th July
The Flowing Brook

Observe a brook gliding through summer meadows, smooth yet persistent as a kingfisher flashes with iridescent splendour above, and let its steady movement remind you that feelings, like water, naturally rise and fall in the rhythm of life. Each mindful pause nurtures calm, patience, and gentle courage, a tranquil balm that soothes even when emotions feel turbulent, like ripples stirred by the kingfisher's dive. Even when feelings surge with intensity, your heart can remain grounded, observing and accepting them with awareness, a quiet poise reflected in the brook's unyielding path. Allow the stream's rhythm to guide your own inner flow, a poetic harmony woven into the fabric of summer's abundance as the waters sing.

Affirmation: Your emotions flow freely, and you meet them with calm, patience, and hope.

19th July
The Sunlit Path of Feeling

A path winds gently through the summer glade,
Shadows and sunlight in a tender cascade.
Your heart moves slowly, step by step,
Acknowledging feelings that quietly crept.
Some are bright, some heavy, some fleeting, some deep,
Each one welcomed, each one to keep.
Breathe in the warmth, the breeze, the air,
Notice emotions without despair.
Even when clouds obscure the light,
Your inner courage shines bright.
Each mindful step, each gentle pause,
Nurtures hope, calm, and quiet cause.
Trust the path, steady and true,
It carries all your feelings and you.
Through sun and shadow, storm and shine,
Your heart learns patience, love, and time.

Affirmation: You meet each emotion with patience, hope, and gentle awareness.

20th July
The Stretch of Summer Light

Let the long sweep of July sunlight warm your shoulders as though you are being slowly welcomed back to yourself. You have moved through seasons of uncertainty and change, learning how to inhabit your body all over again. Today, you need only notice what is here: softness in the air, gold on the grass, breath in your chest. Healing does not always look like leaping forward — sometimes it is simply staying still under the open sky. Trust yourself to blossom at your own pace.

Affirmation: You allow light to enter your life gently and in its own time.

21st July
The Quiet Garden

In the hush of a garden corner, time becomes mercifully unhurried as leaves move without rushing and petals fall without regret, where a snail trails with deliberate slowness across the soil, and you learned long ago that growth is rarely a dramatic affair—more often it happens softly, unseen like the snail's patient path. Today let yourself settle, unforced, among the ordinary miracles of green and growing things that thrive in the summer's warmth, a serene sanctuary of life's quiet beauty. You belong in their company simply by being here, tender-hearted and alive, a poetic harmony woven into the fabric of the garden's embrace.

Affirmation: Your quiet presence honours all the ways you have grown.

22nd July
The River's Rhythm

Watch how the river shines and moves without needing to know where it will end. Its confidence lives in movement, not destination. You too have travelled great stretches of unknowns, learning how to flow with change. Today, trust yourself to drift a little — not driven, not striving, simply responding to what calls you forward. There is wisdom in your pace and beauty in surrendering to the current.

Affirmation: You flow forward with quiet trust in your own rhythm.

23rd July
The Strength of Shade

Under the broad arms of a summer tree, there is sanctuary where shade cools what the sun cannot heal and makes space for rest, as a fox curls with sly repose in the dappled light, and to step back is not to disappear, but to gather your strength among whispering leaves that sigh with the breeze. You have gone through periods of retreat before, not because you were weak but because recovery asked for everything, a tender pause in the summer's warmth. Breathe in this stillness today and remember: to stand in shade is to honour your resilience, a poetic refuge mirrored by the fox's quiet vigilance.

Affirmation: You are still growing, even in safe and shaded places.

24th July
Under the Green Canopy

The canopy sways in lazy July air,
Holding secrets only old trees share.
Branches embrace you without a demand,
Steady and patient, like a quiet hand.
Beneath such leaves you have learned to wait,
To listen for healing, however late.
Not in the rush of the world outside,
But in gentle pauses where hopes abide.
You need not sparkle to prove your worth,
Your very breath belongs to this earth.
Soften your shoulders, loosen your grip,
Let life find you in each rising dip.
For even when weary, unsure, or slow,
You carry more strength than you ever show.
Lie back, and let green shadows tell,
You're safe to just be — and all is well.

Affirmation: You are held exactly where you need to be.

25th July
The Scent of Lavender

A brush of lavender between thumb and forefinger releases a calm that words rarely summon. Sit here for a moment longer than you think you should. Let the fragrance root you in now — not yesterday's trials or tomorrow's worries. There is replenishment in letting your senses be delighted again. Trust that you do not need to go looking for peace; often it finds you softly, through something as small as scent drifting on a summer breeze.

Affirmation: You welcome gentle moments of peace into your day.

26th July
The Butterfly's Rest

Across a sun-baked stone, a butterfly pauses, wings half-open in the heat as a lizard basks with quiet repose nearby, and it knows how to be both delicate and enduring—and so do you, a tender strength that endures through the summer's warmth. Today, let stillness enter you unapologetically, a serene pause in the dance of life, where you are not falling behind but gathering, catching your breath, listening for what wants to emerge next with graceful poise. Rest is not a reward but part of the rhythm of becoming, a poetic harmony mirrored by the butterfly's quiet repose and the lizard's silent vigil.

Affirmation: You allow rest to restore you deeply and without guilt.

27th July
The Hum of Summer

Close your eyes and you can hear summer — bees in clover, distant voices, wind in tall grass. You remember a time when life went on without you, and now you are returning to it slowly, taking your place among ordinary wonders. Let the hum remind you that belonging does not require effort. You need only witness and breathe. That is your contribution: to be here.

Affirmation: You belong gently to the world just as you are.

28th July
Late July Field

Corn stands gold under a watchful sky,
Tall and graceful though storms passed by.
So too have you endured each unknown,
Standing anew where your strength has grown.
Not hurried by time nor claimed by haste,
You rise from seasons you thought you'd waste.
Every whisper of wind against your face
Reminds you gently — you're still in this place.
You do not need to bloom on demand,
Only stand softly, where your life has spanned.
For courage grows quiet in weeks like these,
Among rooted fields and unhurried trees.
Let the month bow round you, wide and bright:
You have become part of summer's light.
Here in the hush of late July's grace,
Feel your own heart fall softly into place.

Affirmation: You rise slowly but surely, just as you are meant to.

29th July
The Evening Sky

The sky deepens from peach to indigo with startling gentleness, a celestial canvas where a firefly flits with silent grace through the twilight, and nothing demands your effort now—not decisions, not optimism, not strength, but instead, you are simply invited to watch colours change and to let yourself be changed in return with poetic serenity. Exhale everything you no longer need to carry, a tender release into the evening's embrace, where peace envelops you like the firefly's quiet flight. There is peace in this evening, and it makes space for who you are becoming, a harmonious hush amid the summer's fading light.

Affirmation: You soften into peace, allowing each breath to carry you further home.

30th July
The Quiet Hills

From the distance, hills look effortless—yet they were shaped by time, weather, and unseen forces as a sheep grazes with placid contentment on the slopes, and you too carry stories of shaping, a tender resilience that stands resolute through the summer's warmth. You may not feel untouched, but you are undeniably present: sturdy, beautiful, quietly majestic in your perseverance, a poetic testament to endurance mirrored by the sheep's quiet vigil. Stand where you are and feel the earth beneath your soles, a grounding embrace that whispers of your strength—you are not broken; you are formed with graceful poise amid the rolling landscape.

Affirmation: You honour the strength in the contours of your own becoming.

31st July — Monthly Reflection Poem
July's Quiet Strength

July held you in a cradle of light,
Long afternoons, soft breathing at night.
You learned to pause without the race,
To find yourself in a still, safe place.
Some mornings bright as a child's delight,
Some evenings heavy yet deeply right.
You watched leaves tremble and stars appear,
Letting each moment draw you near.
What you endured now turns to grace,
You carry it softly in heart-held space.
There's tenderness now where once was fight,
A quieter way of holding your might.
Step into August with gentle heart,
Knowing your healing is living art.
Not finished, not hurried, but steady and wise,
Strong as hills beneath summer skies.

Affirmation: You carry your strength softly, trusting in all you have become.

AUGUST

1st August – Monthly Opening Poem

August's Golden Invitation

Sunlight stretches, honeyed and slow,
Over fields where wildflowers grow.
The air is thick with warmth and ease,
A gentle balm that whispers, "Breathe."
Each day invites you to step outside,
To watch the light in streams collide.
Evening drapes the hills in gold,
A story of resilience quietly told.
Let the breeze remind you to soften,
To let your pace be slow, yet often.
Nature does not rush, nor does it strain,
It simply exists, enduring each rain.
Take heart in this subtle, steady flow,
And allow your own quiet courage to show.
August calls you to pause, to see,
The beauty of being simply free.

Affirmation: You welcome this month with gentle hope and quiet joy.

2nd August
The Morning Light

The sun wakes slowly over the orchard, spilling gold across dewy leaves. Notice how the light touches each branch and fruit, unhurried and patient. Your own mornings can mirror this pace: soft, careful, a gentle unfolding. You do not need to arrive anywhere; you simply arrive as yourself. Let each breath be like sunlight warming your chest, small yet persistent. Even quiet moments carry meaning when you meet them fully. Today, move with curiosity and wonder, letting life's light find you.

Affirmation: You rise each day into gentle warmth and quiet strength.

3rd August
The Whispering Meadow

Grass bends under the weight of the summer breeze, murmuring secrets only you can hear. You have learned to listen carefully to what your body and heart whisper. Notice small wonders — a bee pausing, a cloud drifting slowly, the hum of life around you. Every breath, every step, is a reminder of resilience that often goes unseen. There is magic in simplicity; even the ordinary becomes extraordinary when fully noticed. Let this meadow guide you to a soft, open awareness, grounding your mind and spirit. You are part of this gentle rhythm, moving in harmony with what surrounds you.

Affirmation: You are attentive to the quiet beauty and strength around you.

4th August
The Cool of Trees

Step beneath the generous shade of an old oak or maple. Notice how the leaves filter light into dancing patterns on the ground. Just as the branches bend without breaking, you too have the flexibility to endure, to rest, to sway. The heat of summer reminds you to slow down, to drink deeply, to simply exist. Even small pauses carry meaning — a sip of water, a breath of air, a long exhale. Nature's patience teaches you that steady growth and gentle resilience are enough. Today, let yourself rest in the quiet, held by green branches above.

Affirmation: You are supported by the quiet strength that surrounds you.

5th August
The Silver Stream

A stream slips over stones, murmuring in soft silver tones. Its movement is effortless, yet persistent, shaping everything it touches. Notice how your own life flows similarly, with moments of stillness and moments of progress. Even when things seem slow, they are moving in ways you may not yet see. The light catches on the water, sparkling as if to remind you of hidden joys. Pause here, and feel the steady rhythm in your chest, in your steps, in your breath. There is magic in persistence, quiet but undeniable, carrying life forward.

Affirmation: You trust the gentle flow of your own journey.

6th August
The Evening Glow

The sky glows amber as day gives way to dusk, softening the edges of the world. Evening has a way of inviting stillness, encouraging reflection and quiet gratitude. Notice the warmth lingering on rooftops, leaves, and hillsides — it holds you too. Let the softness of twilight remind you that not all endings are harsh; some simply invite rest. Breathe deeply, feeling the slow exhale of the day leaving your chest. You are part of this ebb and flow, a living reflection of light and calm. Tonight, allow the day's gentle surrender to soothe and renew you.

Affirmation: You find comfort in the quiet closure of each day.

7th August
The Fields of Late Summer

Fields sway golden beneath the sun's warm gaze,
Rippling softly in a summer haze.
You have walked these paths of quiet trial,
And now you linger a moment, taking in the mile.
Sunflowers nod, bright and tall,
Reminding you that patience encompasses all.
Even in days of waiting, there is grace,
Visible in wind's touch, sunlight's embrace.
Your journey is layered, subtle, and true,
As are the fields unfolding beneath skies of blue.
Notice the warmth on your skin, the hum in the air,
Life continues to move, tender and fair.
Step softly, breathe fully, embrace what's near,
Let each golden stalk remind you to be here.
Your strength lives quietly, yet entirely clear.

Affirmation: You are present and strong, nourished by the world around you.

8th August
The Meadow's Song

Wildflowers lift their faces to the sun, each petal a small triumph. Notice how even the smallest bloom contributes beauty without effort. Your own efforts, quiet or bold, ripple out in ways unseen. Even in moments of fatigue, you have a presence that matters. Listen to the meadow: birds, wind, distant laughter — it sings softly of life. Let your heart rise in tune with these subtle harmonies. You are allowed to exist fully here, in this warmth, in this calm.

Affirmation: You recognise your presence as a quiet, enduring gift.

9th August
The Golden Path

A sunlit path winds between tall grasses, inviting steps that are unhurried. Notice how each step matters simply because it is taken. You have learned to pace yourself, to respect what your body and spirit need. The warmth on your shoulders reminds you of resilience — steady, patient, sure. Allow your eyes to drink in the colour and light around you, grounding each breath. Even as days stretch long, there is beauty in small, mindful movements. Walk softly today, knowing that your rhythm is enough.

Affirmation: You move at a pace that honours your journey.

10th August
The Honeyed Breeze

A gentle breeze stirs the lavender and rosemary, carrying hints of distant hills. Feel how the wind moves through your hair, across your face, into your lungs. Even subtle changes bring reassurance: air, warmth, life. Notice how the natural world bends and sways without resistance, teaching grace. Take this moment to inhale deeply, noticing strength returning in quiet ways. Today, the breeze carries you gently, reminding you to soften, to be present. There is lightness in your steps, if you allow it to touch you.

Affirmation: You welcome life's gentle currents into your heart.

11th August
The Riverbend

Behold the water curving around a quiet bend, its silver-blue pools reflecting clouds and sky with ethereal grace as an otter glides with silent elegance along its banks, and notice how it moves—neither fast nor slow—simply as it is meant to, a poetic dance of nature's timeless rhythm. Your own path, with its gentle turns and thoughtful pauses, mirrors this natural cadence, a serene flow through the late summer landscape where a kingfisher darts with iridescent splendour above. Even when the way ahead veils itself in uncertainty, there is guidance in observing the river's steady course, in listening to its soft murmur that whispers of resilience amid the rustling reeds. You have learned patience, strength, and quiet resilience, a tender strength woven into the fabric of your soul, and step lightly today, letting your mind float on the calm surface, a harmonious drift guided by the otter's graceful presence. The river teaches that movement itself is enough, a sacred lesson carried on the warm August breeze.

Affirmation: You trust the natural rhythm of your own life.

12th August
The Sun on Leaves

Sunlight warms the green canopy, dappling leaves in shimmering patterns. Notice how life continues its quiet, patient dance around you. Even small sparks of light bring clarity and gentle joy. Allow your senses to linger, to marvel without agenda. You are part of this rhythm, contributing without needing to change. Let warmth fill your chest and spread to your shoulders and back. Even fleeting moments of delight remind you that life can be soft and full.

Affirmation: You receive the world's quiet gifts with openness and gratitude.

13th August
The Late Afternoon Meadow

Time stretches lazily across fields and meadows, settling into warmth. You too can stretch, allowing your body and mind to linger. Notice the hum of bees, the drift of cloud shadows, the slow sway of grass. Even a single hour can be rich with attention and presence. Today, take comfort in the small details, in the ordinary miracles of life. Step lightly, breathe deeply, and let your spirit rest in this moment. All that is required is simply to notice and be.

Affirmation: You inhabit each moment fully and gently.

14th August
The Late Summer Light

Golden light spills over hill and vale,
Soft and warm as a whispered tale.
Grass bows lightly to the passing breeze,
Carrying the hum of hidden bees.
You have wandered, sometimes tired and slow,
Yet find strength in the paths you know.
The sun remincs you of gentle power,
Even in the quietest summer hour.
Rivers shimmer, reflecting sky above,
Teaching persistence without shove.
Every leaf, every bloom, every sound,
Holds a whisper that strength is around.
Let warmth settle deep in your chest,
Feel the calm in the world's slow rest.
You are part of this rhythm, complete and true,
A light in the late summer, soft and new.

Affirmation: You carry quiet strength, steady and enduring.

15th August
The Quiet Path

Wander along a shaded trail where sunlight scatters through leaves with golden grace, its dappled rays illuminating the late summer woodland as a thrush serenades with resonant melody from a nearby bough, each step a gentle reminder of the journey you've traversed with tender resilience. Some roads have stretched long and winding, their bends unexpected like the twists of a deer's path through the undergrowth, yet here you stand, moving with your own quiet strength, a poetic harmony woven into the fabric of nature's embrace. Let the birdsong fill the spaces that once felt empty, its lilting notes a balm carried on the warm August breeze, soothing the soul with the thrush's vigilant presence. Even in stillness, you carry forward, unseen but steady, a silent force mirrored by the deer's graceful stride, your spirit resilient amid the rustling leaves. Today, trust the path and the pace that suits your own rhythm, a sacred cadence guided by the woodland's timeless serenity.

Affirmation: You move forward with quiet resilience and grace.

16th August
The Honeyed Hills

Hills glow in the late afternoon, soft against the horizon. Notice their patient curves, shaped by seasons and time. You too have been shaped by forces unseen, yet here you stand. Even small victories count: a breath fully drawn, a quiet smile, a moment of ease in the warmth of summer light. Let the gentle hills remind you that persistence is beautiful, and that your strength has quietly grown with every day.

Affirmation: You honour the strength that has formed in silence.

17th August
The Lavender Breeze

A soft wind stirs the lavender and grasses along the field's edge. Even the smallest movement can awaken senses dulled by the past. Notice how the scent carries across the summer air, subtle, persistent, calming your mind without effort. There is something sacred in returning to small joys, in letting the world remind you of life's gentle pleasures. Today, allow yourself to linger in this quiet restoration.

Affirmation: You welcome gentle refreshment into your spirit.

18th August
The Sunlit Clearing

Step into a clearing where sunlight falls freely, its golden rays cascading through the late summer canopy as a deer pauses with serene grace amid the tall grasses, and let the warmth touch the places within your soul that yearn for its gentle embrace, a tender balm in the August stillness. Some days call for a pause, a reverent stillness mirrored by the deer's quiet vigil, while others allow movement, a dance with the breeze that rustles the leaves, yet every moment carries a lesson of renewal woven into nature's timeless rhythm. Notice the way light moves through branches and over grass, its radiant fingers illuminating the earth with patience and steady care, a poetic reflection of resilience amid the woodland's embrace. Reflect upon this clarity that bathes the clearing, where a blackbird sings with mellifluous charm, and today, breathe in the serenity that light provides, a sacred breath that nurtures your spirit under the summer sky.

Affirmation: You accept each moment of warmth and renewal.

19th August
The Rippled Pond

A pond catches the sky and folds it gently into its surface. Ripples move outward, small and unassuming, yet persistent. Your own life has sent ripples across days, subtle reminders that presence, patience, and care matter. Even quiet progress counts toward something larger. Take a long breath, feeling the steady rhythm within yourself, and notice the reflection of growth in your own calm.

Affirmation: You trust the quiet, steady currents of your life.

20th August
The Summer Meadow

Golden flowers sway in the afternoon light, their petals lifting and falling with natural grace. You, too, have experienced cycles of energy and stillness, and find yourself returning, each day, to the simple act of being. Notice the gentle hum of life around you: insects, wind, distant laughter. Even small attentions nourish the soul in ways unseen. Today, let yourself be fully present in the meadow's soft embrace.

Affirmation: You flourish quietly, in your own time and space.

21st August
The River's Edge

Water winds lazily over smooth stones, reflecting sun and sky. It flows without hurry, yet it reaches every corner it touches. You move through life in similar, steady ways, adapting, bending, yet persisting with quiet strength. Notice the shimmer of light across the surface, a gentle reminder that resilience is reflected in subtle ways. Step beside the river today and let its calm shape your own rhythm.

Affirmation: You allow your strength to emerge softly, naturally.

22nd August
The Whispering Trees

Behold tall trees swaying in the warm summer breeze, their leaves murmuring ancient tales of seasons past as a squirrel leaps with nimble grace from branch to branch, a poetic symphony of resilience woven into the late summer air. Even when branches have been battered by tempests, they remain upright, their trunks a testament to endurance, growing quietly stronger with each day that passes under the golden canopy, mirrored by the squirrel's steadfast dance. Notice how their patience mirrors your own quiet endurance, a gentle reminder that recovery and growth unfold with the tender rhythm of nature, a sacred dance amid the rustling foliage. Today, breathe in the whispers that drift through the leaves, feel their steady encouragement as a blackbird sings with mellifluous charm nearby, a serene breath that nurtures your spirit in the embrace of the woodland's timeless strength.

Affirmation: You grow stronger each day, in ways that may be unseen.

23rd August
The Late Summer Light

Sunlight drapes over the fields and hills,
Softly touching flowers, leaves, and rills.
The breeze carries warmth without demand,
Guiding life gently across the land.
You have walked paths both smooth and rough,
Learning patience, courage, and quiet love.
Every day's journey, subtle yet profound,
Leaves a mark in ways that may not resound.
The hum of bees, the shimmer of grass,
Remind you that time allows you to pass
Through challenge, through pause, through soft renewal,
Each moment shaping your own gentle renewal.
You are part of this light, tender and bright,
A presence in late summer, steady and right.
Carry this calm into all the days ahead,
Let it nourish your heart, your thoughts, your stead.

Affirmation: You are part of a quiet, enduring strength.

24th August
The Golden Hills

Hillsides glow in fading sunlight, rich with late-summer warmth. Notice how they rise and fall effortlessly, enduring seasons, storms, and stillness. Your own life mirrors this rhythm, softly, without fanfare. Even moments of pause carry meaning, allowing your strength to grow quietly. Step slowly today, feeling the earth beneath your feet, and notice how calm, steady attention becomes its own power. You are rooted, yet flexible, enduring, yet light.

Affirmation: You move through life with steady grace and quiet power.

25th August
The Gentle Brook

A brook winds between stones, singing softly in the afternoon sun. Its flow is persistent, but never hurried; its purpose gentle. Even in still waters there is motion beneath the surface. Your own life has ebbs and flows, quiet and strong. Notice the shimmer of the water and the way light bends upon it, reflecting hope, calm, and persistence in subtle ways. Today, walk beside this brook and feel your spirit's steady rhythm.

Affirmation: You embrace the subtle, enduring flow of your life.

26th August
The Warm Breeze

Let the late summer breeze waft through the air, bearing scents of grass, hay, and distant flowers, a fragrant ode carried on its gentle wings as a butterfly dances with delicate grace amid the wild blooms, a poetic embrace of nature's late August splendour. Feel it as it brushes your skin with tender warmth, a reminder of life's small pleasures that linger like the butterfly's fleeting touch, awakening your spirit to the day's quiet beauty. Even when energy feels fleeting, like the fading light of a summer evening, notice how warmth can still enter, a serene gift mirrored by a hare pausing with vigilant poise in the meadow. Pause and inhale deeply, letting subtle joy fill your chest, a harmonious breath that rises with the breeze, while the world continues in its gentle rhythm, inviting you to move with it as the hare bounds softly onward. Today, allow this breeze to refresh your spirit and restore your calm, a sacred renewal woven into the fabric of the landscape, affirming that you are part of this gentle, persistent vitality that hums through the earth.

Affirmation: You are renewed by the quiet gifts of the world.

27th August
The Meadow Path

A narrow path winds through tall summer grasses, dappled with sunlight. Step lightly, noticing each leaf, each sound, each gentle sway. You have travelled far, and yet this small path reminds you of quiet presence. Every step counts, whether bold or tentative, fast or slow. Even brief pauses carry significance, revealing strength that rests unseen. Move through the meadow with awareness, letting nature guide your rhythm. You are exactly where you need to be, in harmony with the day.

Affirmation: You move forward gently, guided by your own inner rhythm.

28th August
The Gilded Meadow

Sunlight drapes over the late summer fields,
Every stalk of grain a story it yields.
The wind whispers softly through each blade,
Reminding you of quiet progress made.
You have faced long days and nights of pause,
Yet still, you move with gentle cause.
Even small victories are worthy of praise,
And subtle strength deserves patient gaze.
The hum of life continues, calm and steady,
Its rhythm persistent, simple, and ready.
Notice how light bends across leaf and flower,
Teaching that strength grows in quiet hours.
You are part of this tapestry, subtle and bright,
Living proof of persistence, courage, and light.
Let the late summer sun warm your chest,
And feel your heart quietly, fully blessed.

Affirmation: You flourish in gentle, enduring ways.

29th August
The Evening Glow

Behold as dusk softens the edges of the world, brushing the skies with lilac and rose, a celestial canvas where a bat flits with silent grace through the twilight, and notice the calm settling over the land and within your soul, a poetic hush that envelops the late summer evening. Even brief pauses, like the bat's fleeting dance, allow healing and reflection to take hold, a tender balm woven into the fabric of the fading light as a fox pauses with sly elegance in the distance. Breathe slowly, letting the warmth of this gentle glow fill your chest, a serene breath that rises with the evening's embrace, mirroring the fox's quiet vigil amid the rustling grasses. Today, you are invited to simply rest, to witness the world's tranquil unfolding, and to be, a sacred communion with nature's rhythm under the August sky. No hurry, no pressure, only the quiet passage of time, a harmonious cadence that soothes the spirit, and let the evening's gentle glow remind you of resilience and ease, a radiant promise carried on the breeze.

Affirmation: You rest in the soft light of your own presence.

30th August
The Hills at Twilight

Hills stand in silhouette, their curves softened by twilight. Look at them, and see how even the tallest forms yield to light and shadow. Your own journey has been shaped by unseen hands, yet you endure. Notice how calm descends, steadying the mind and heart. Each step, each breath, each quiet pause builds subtle strength. You are capable of stillness as well as motion, softness as well as persistence. Stand gently, noticing how peace and courage coexist in your chest.

Affirmation: You carry calm and resilience together, naturally and freely.

31st August — Monthly Reflection Poem
August's Golden Embrace

August carried you in warmth and light,
Softly guiding from morning into night.
You walked through quiet meadows and fields of gold,
Gathering strength that will quietly hold.
Some days were bright, others tempered with pause,
Yet each brought you closer to your own gentle cause.
Breezes whispered, rivers reflected the sky,
Teaching patience, persistence, and how to simply try.
Even in still moments, your spirit was present,
Finding subtle victories, gentle and effervescent.
The late summer sun glowed over hills and trees,
Reminding you of resilience that moves like the breeze.
Carry this light into September and beyond,
Knowing your own rhythm is steady, steadfast, and strong.
You have flourished softly, like fields under golden skies,
And may your heart continue to hold this quiet prize.

Affirmation: You move forward with grace, strength, and gentle hope.

SEPTEMBER

1st September – Monthly Opening Poem

September's Gentle Call

Leaves turn gently, gold and amber bright,
As summer fades into softer light.
Each day invites a moment to pause,
To notice life's subtle, quiet laws.
Evening drapes the trees in mellow glow,
A time for calm, reflection to flow.
Change moves slowly, yet with purpose clear,
Teaching patience, resilience year by year.
Step with care, each gesture tender and small,
Embrace the quiet, the beauty of it all.
Let your heart open to gentle transition,
Trust the strength that dwells in quiet vision.
Every breath, each shifting beam of light,
Holds a lesson in hope, steady and bright.
September whispers softly, calm and true,
"I hold resilience and gentle strength for you."

Affirmation: You welcome change with gentle curiosity and calm strength.

2nd September
The Crisp Morning

A cool autumn breeze brushes your cheeks as the day begins, carrying the scent of turning leaves and distant earth. The sun, softened by the season, warms without overwhelming, reminding you of gentle balance. Today, pause to notice small details: the shimmer of dew on grass, the subtle rustle of leaves overhead, and the quiet rhythm of your own breathing. Even amidst uncertainty, there is resilience in simply showing up, in continuing your journey with care. Let your thoughts drift softly, acknowledging what is, without judgement, and allow nature's calm to mirror the quiet steadiness within you. Each step, however small, is a part of your forward motion.

Affirmation: You move through change with patience, grace, and awareness.

3rd September
The Golden Meadow

Sunlight stretches low across fields turning gold, and shadows lengthen softly beneath the trees. Notice the way autumn light transforms the world, revealing beauty in subtle change. Life unfolds in its own rhythm, and your own journey mirrors this natural ebb and flow, blending moments of stillness with gentle movement. Today, take time to linger in observation, letting the warmth of the light and the quiet rustle of leaves guide your calm and restore your spirit. Every small sign of life and growth is a reminder of the subtle strength within you, present even when unseen.

Affirmation: You find hope and steadiness in life's shifting rhythms.

4th September
The Whispering Trees

The trees murmur softly in the wind, their branches swaying in patient endurance. Even when change feels uncertain or slow, there is strength in simply standing, rooted yet flexible. Let their quiet resilience reflect your own, offering gentle reassurance. Walk through your day with awareness, feeling the balance between movement and stillness, effort and rest. Today, notice the soft interplay of light and shadow, of cool and warmth, and allow it to mirror the rhythm of your own journey. Each gentle sway of the branches is a subtle invitation to trust in yourself and the unfolding path.

Affirmation: You embrace life's transitions with courage and ease.

5th September
The Stream's Reflection

A clear stream winds through the meadow, glinting under soft sunlight and flowing effortlessly around stones. Its steady movement reminds you that life moves at its own pace, sometimes quietly, sometimes with gentle turbulence. Even small ripples carry meaning, and even slow currents shape the land. Notice how your journey has its own ebb and flow, each turn and pause forming a pattern of resilience. Today, let your awareness drift with the stream, attuning to the balance of motion and stillness, and notice the subtle strength that carries you forward, gently and persistently.

Affirmation: You trust the quiet current of your own journey.

6th September
The Harvest Breeze

The air is fragrant with the soft scent of ripening fields, earthy and warm. Breezes drift through trees, ruffling leaves and carrying subtle reminders of change and growth. Even small pauses allow reflection and nourishment, and each quiet moment can replenish your strength. Today, move through your surroundings with awareness, noticing the golden light, the hum of insects, and the soft rustle of grass underfoot. Let these small, sustaining details remind you of the steady rhythm that underpins your journey and the hope that resides in gentle observation.

Affirmation: You are nourished by the world's subtle, sustaining gifts.

7th September
Autumn's Gentle Whisper

Golden leaves drift down from patient trees,
Dancing lightly in the soft September breeze.
The sun tilts lower, painting fields in amber hue,
And every day unfolds with something new.
You have faced seasons both warm and cold,
Yet here you stand, quietly strong and bold.
Even when paths were hidden, uncertain, or long,
You learned that quiet courage can carry you along.
Notice the way light filters through fading green,
Shining on moments unseen, yet serene.
Every gentle shift, every subtle change,
Shapes your rhythm, steady and strange.
The world reminds you to bend, to sway, to rest,
To recognise the progress quietly expressed.
Step lightly, breathe fully, let your spirit expand,
And notice resilience held softly in your hand.

Affirmation: You are steady, resilient, and open to life's unfolding.

8th September
The Early Dawn

Mist settles over fields as morning stretches into light, bringing a cool hush and a sense of possibility. Even if yesterday felt heavy, today offers quiet renewal. Take a moment to notice the shimmer of dew, the soft golden edge of sunlight, and the gentle stirrings of life waking around you. Each breath is an invitation to move with calm awareness, attuning to the rhythms of your own body and the world outside. Let the quiet freshness of dawn fill you with subtle hope and steady energy for the day ahead.

Affirmation: Each morning renews your courage and inner peace.

9th September
The Amber Path

A winding path stretches through the trees, their leaves turning warm shades of amber and rust. The soft crunch beneath your feet reminds you that even small steps matter and that gentle progress has its own rhythm. Notice the light and shadow playing across the forest floor, and let this quiet contrast mirror the subtle balance in your own journey. Today, walk mindfully, appreciating each curve and each moment, and trust that your pace is exactly what is needed to carry you forward with calm confidence.

Affirmation: You move forward with mindful ease and grace.

10th September
The Calm River

The river glides smoothly past stones, catching soft autumn light and reflecting the sky above. Even the gentlest currents shape the shore, a reminder that quiet persistence matters. Your journey has its own patterns, with pauses and gentle surges, and each carries meaning. Today, observe the steady flow, the soft murmur of water, and allow it to inspire patience and trust in your own path. Every ripple, however subtle, contributes to the larger picture, just as your steady efforts do.

Affirmation: You trust in your own patient, steady resilience.

11th September
The Orchard's Edge

Fruit hangs heavy on branches, bright against the softening light of September afternoons. Leaves whisper in the breeze, bending without breaking, reminding you of quiet endurance. Take time to notice the richness around you—the texture of bark, the gentle sway of branches, the warm scent of ripening fruit—and let it mirror the strength within yourself. Today, move slowly, absorbing the details of the orchard and finding reassurance in the enduring rhythm of nature, carrying its calm and resilience into your own day.

Affirmation: You acknowledge and honour your enduring courage.

12th September
The Sunlit Clearing

Step into a sunlit clearing where light pools softly on the grass, and shadows stretch long and calm. Even brief moments of stillness allow reflection, and subtle energy returns to your chest. Notice how the sunlight filters through leaves, highlighting the quiet textures and gentle colours of the season. Today, let this light guide your thoughts and spirit, a reminder that change can be gentle and sustaining, and that hope persists quietly alongside each shift in life's rhythm.

> Affirmation: You welcome light and calm into your heart.

13th September
The Forest Floor

Leaves gather in rich, textured layers beneath tall trees, forming a carpet of amber, ochre, and soft decay. Each layer feeds the next, creating life even in what seems still. Your own journey has similar rhythms, with cycles of challenge and renewal, and subtle progress builds quietly, without fanfare. Walk slowly today, aware of every step and every small detail, listening to the hum of life around you, and let the forest floor remind you of the steady growth and quiet strength that persist even when unseen.

> Affirmation: You find growth and renewal in every step forward.

14th September
September's Golden Drift

Leaves drift softly through the mellow air,
Gold, amber, and russet, floating without care.
The sun dips lower, bathing fields in warm light,
Yet mornings bring mist, soft and bright.
You have traversed seasons both gentle and wild,
Each day shaping your body, your heart, and your mind.
Even in times of uncertainty, you have persisted,
Finding strength in quiet moments, softly insisted.
Rivers hum and hills breathe under skies wide,
Teaching patience, endurance, and the calm inside.
Every leaf that falls carries subtle grace,
A gentle reminder that change has its own pace.
Step lightly, breathe fully, let your spirit expand,
Notice resilience held softly in your hand.
September drifts onward, tender and clear,
And hope remains close, quietly near.

Affirmation: You embrace change with grace, strength, and gentle hope.

15th September
The Soft Horizon

The horizon glows with amber and soft rose as the day begins, a gentle reminder that each moment carries subtle beauty. Trees sway slowly in the breeze, leaves brushing softly against one another, echoing your own quiet resilience. Today, notice how the world moves at its own pace, and how even gentle effort sustains progress. Let yourself follow the rhythm of nature, pausing when needed, moving when ready, and embracing both light and shadow. The season reminds you that change can be gradual, steady, and beautiful, and that your own journey mirrors this balance.

Affirmation: You move through life with patience, grace, and gentle awareness.

16th September
The Sunlit Stream

A narrow stream glints under the soft September sun, rippling around stones and carrying leaves along its current. Watch how the water flows steadily, shaping its path without rush or complaint. Even small shifts in direction matter, and every gentle movement contributes to its course. Today, let the stream remind you that forward motion can be quiet and patient, and that your own persistence is seen in subtle but meaningful ways. Take time to notice the light sparkling on the surface, the hum of life along the banks, and the calm reassurance that steady progress brings.

Affirmation: You trust the gentle, patient flow of your journey.

17th September
The Amber Canopy

Walking beneath a canopy of leaves turned gold, red, and ochre, you feel the subtle whisper of change in the air. Light filters softly through branches, illuminating the path ahead and reflecting the shifts within yourself. Each step is an opportunity to notice beauty and embrace the slow transformations around you. Let the play of light and shadow remind you that growth often happens quietly, unseen, yet always present. Today, breathe deeply, moving with awareness, and carry this gentle steadiness into your thoughts, your actions, and your heart.

Affirmation: You are resilient and attuned to life's quiet transformations.

18th September
The Meadow's Edge

Wander along the meadow's edge where tall grasses sway in the breeze, brushing your fingertips with tender grace as a hare bounds with quiet elegance through the golden fronds, the air scented with earth, late blooms, and a hint of the coming autumn chill that whispers of change in the late summer light. Notice the rhythm of the meadow, the way each stem bends without breaking under the wind's caress, and let it mirror the patience and flexibility blossoming within your soul, a poetic harmony woven into nature's enduring embrace. Today, walk slowly, savouring the subtle textures—the velvet of petals, the rustle of leaves—where a blackbird sings with mellifluous charm, and behold the interplay of light and shadow dancing across the landscape, a tender encouragement from the natural world. Each small observation carries calm and hope, a serene gift reflected in the hare's vigilant poise, reminding you that growth and renewal unfold at their own gentle pace, a sacred cadence amid the fading warmth of September's eve.

Affirmation: You move forward with gentle strength and awareness.

19th September
The Quiet Hills

Gaze upon hills rising softly in the distance, wrapped in warm golden light that bathes the late summer landscape as a skylark ascends with joyous melody above their gentle slopes, a testament to persistence and grace etched into nature's fading embrace. The wind carries a subtle freshness, brushing across your face with tender caress and filling your chest with calm, where a hare pauses with serene poise amid the swaying grasses, its breath a poetic harmony with the earth's quiet rhythm. Today, allow your thoughts to follow the curves of the landscape, noticing how each rise and fall reflects your own journey, a tender dance mirrored by the skylark's soaring flight and the hare's steadfast path through the golden hues. Even when paths seem uncertain, veiled in the mists of doubt as autumn whispers near, steady steps build resilience, a gentle strength woven into the fabric of your soul, while quiet observation restores balance, a sacred pause amid the rolling hills. Let the hills remind you that progress does not need to be loud; it can be patient, measured, and enduring, a radiant promise carried on the September breeze as the day softens into twilight.

Affirmation: You trust your own steady, resilient pace.

20th September
The Woodland Path

A narrow path winds through trees shedding their first autumn leaves, creating a soft carpet of amber underfoot. Listen to the gentle rustle with every step and feel the way the air shifts with movement. Change occurs naturally, like the shedding of leaves, and your own journey mirrors this rhythm. Today, notice how light filters through the branches, how shadows stretch and contract, and allow these subtle signs to guide your reflection and calm. Each step carries quiet affirmation that resilience and hope are always present, even in gentle, unseen ways.

Affirmation: You embrace each step with mindful presence and quiet courage.

21st September
September's Gentle Flow

Leaves fall softly on the forest floor,
Whispering stories of what came before.
Light filters gently through ambered trees,
And dances along the path with ease.
The wind bends branches but does not break,
A lesson in resilience for your own sake.
Rivers hum under skies wide and clear,
Carrying whispers of hope for those who hear.
Every step you take, every breath you claim,
Adds to the quiet strength that cannot wane.
Even in change, even in the unseen,
There is beauty, patience, and moments between.
Step lightly, breathe fully, embrace the calm,
And let nature's rhythm be your balm.
September moves onward, tender and bright,
Guiding your heart with gentle, steady light.

Affirmation: You are guided by quiet strength and natural rhythm.

22nd September
The Dewed Grass

Morning dew glistens on soft green blades, catching the first light like tiny lanterns. Each droplet mirrors the subtle reflection of your own resilience, quietly sustaining you. Today, move slowly through the day, noticing small details—a soft breeze, a bird in flight, the warmth of sunlight on your hands—and let them remind you of the gentle strength within. Nature's quiet rhythms teach patience, steady growth, and hope that is always present, even when unseen.

Affirmation: You find calm and encouragement in life's quiet details.

23rd September
The Orchard Path

Branches hang low with late-season fruit, bending without breaking under their weight. Observe the balance between effort and ease, and let it reflect your own ability to endure and thrive. The scent of ripening apples and fading blossoms fills the air, a reminder that beauty accompanies persistence. Today, walk with awareness, noticing every soft texture, the interplay of sun and shadow, and the gentle encouragement of the world around you. Each step affirms your resilience and your capacity to move forward with grace.

Affirmation: You are strengthened by the balance of patience and persistence.

24th September
The Gentle Hillside

Soft slopes rise into the distance, their tops bathed in amber light and their shadows stretching long across the valley. Notice how the terrain undulates, inviting slow, mindful movement. Today, observe how the gentle inclines and curves mirror your own journey, with quiet progress and subtle strength. Let your steps be intentional, your breath steady, and your heart open to the beauty of natural rhythms. In small motions, you will find reassurance, patience, and hope.

Affirmation: You move with gentle awareness, guided by calm and inner strength.

25th September
The Quiet Stream

A narrow stream flows with serene persistence, weaving through reeds and around small stones. Observe how each ripple contributes to the shaping of the land, reminding you that even subtle efforts have lasting impact. Today, let the stream inspire patience and trust in your own journey. Notice the sparkle of sunlight on water, the hum of life along the banks, and the quiet assurance that your resilience continues to grow.

Affirmation: You trust in your steady, patient progress through life.

26th September
The Forest Light

Sunlight filters through a canopy of turning leaves, creating dappled patterns on the forest floor. Each patch of light illuminates what was hidden, inviting awareness and reflection. Today, notice how illumination comes gradually, and how small shifts in perception bring understanding and calm. Allow the gentle play of light and shadow to remind you of the resilience and hope quietly present within yourself. Move slowly, breathe fully, and embrace the subtle changes around and within you.

Affirmation: You welcome insight and calm with patience and trust.

27th September
The Meadow Breeze

A soft wind stirs grasses and late blooms, carrying the scent of earth and distant trees. Feel the soft wind stirring grasses and late blooms, its tender breath carrying the scent of earth and distant trees as a hedgehog rustles with quiet purpose through the undergrowth, a poetic whisper of autumn's gentle embrace in the waning summer light. Let this graceful movement remind you of your own capacity for flexibility and endurance, a resilient dance mirrored by the hedgehog's steady journey amid the golden fronds, where unseen shifts weave strength into the fabric of your soul. Even quiet, unseen transformations contribute to growth and change, a sacred rhythm reflected in the meadow's fading splendour as a skylark ascends with joyous melody above. Today, move with awareness of the natural cadence around you, noticing the interplay of wind rustling through leaves, light dappling the earth, and shadow stretching across the landscape, a harmonious interplay that reinforces your calm, steady resilience. Each small observation nurtures hope and balance, a tender gift carried on the September breeze as the day softens into twilight's serene hush.

Affirmation: You are carried forward by life's subtle, sustaining rhythms.

28th September
Autumn's Steady Song

Amber leaves drift through the gentle air,
Turning slowly, floating without care.
The sun rests low, warming field and tree,
Painting soft reflections for all who see.
Paths twist through hills both near and far,
Reminding you of how steady you are.
Rivers hum under skies wide and deep,
Carrying whispers of hope you can keep.
Even in change, even in quiet unseen,
There is persistence, patience, and steady routine.
Every leaf that falls, every soft breeze,
Speaks of endurance and moments of ease.
Step lightly, breathe fully, feel the earth's calm,
Embrace the warmth of its comforting balm.
September's song is steady and true,
Guiding your heart as it carries you through.

Affirmation: You are resilient, patient, and guided by hope.

29th September
The Orchard in Light

Branches glow in amber light, carrying fruit heavy with the season's bounty. Each bend and sway teaches gentle endurance, and each subtle shift reminds you of the quiet strength within. Today, notice the textures, colours, and scent of the orchard around you, letting these details restore your sense of calm and balance. The season encourages reflection and patience, and even small, mindful observations carry meaning and hope.

Affirmation: You find strength and calm in life's quiet rhythms.

30th September – Monthly Reflection Poem
September's Gentle Lessons

Leaves tumble softly in the amber light,
Whispering stories of day and night.
The sun dips lower, yet mornings bring glow,
Mists rise slowly over fields below.
Rivers hum through valleys serene,
Carrying whispers of all that has been.
The forest breathes in rhythm with you,
Teaching patience in all that you do.
Even unseen progress is shaping the way,
Small steps and quiet moments hold sway.
Breezes bend branches without breaking,
Every leaf and shadow a lesson in taking
Time to rest, to move, to observe, to see,
That resilience and hope flow patiently.
September departs with gentle cheer,
Leaving your heart steady, calm, and clear.

Affirmation: You embrace life's rhythm with grace, patience, and quiet hope.

OCTOBER

1st October – Monthly Opening Poem

October's Gentle Embrace

October arrives with skies of gold,
A soft light brushing stories untold.
Leaves drift slowly, crisp and bright,
Whispering courage in morning light.
Even when the air feels cold and still,
Hope and strength bloom at your will.
Each breath you take, each gentle stride,
Carries warmth and calm deep inside.
Let the winds of change guide your heart,
Bringing renewal, a brand-new start.
October whispers, tender and true,
"I hold resilience and hope for you."
Embrace this month with gentle grace,
And feel the peace that fills your space.

Affirmation: You welcome the gentle rhythms of October into your heart.

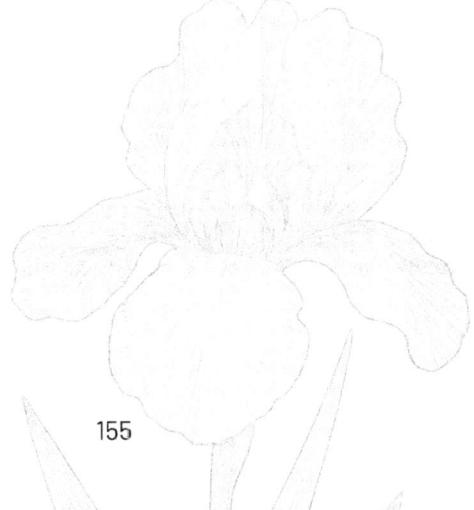

2nd October
The Strength in Stillness

There is quiet power in stillness, a sacred space where your spirit can breathe and your heart can soften. Today, pause deliberately to listen to the subtle whispers of your inner wisdom, to honour the small movements of your body, and to simply be present. In this gentle pause, notice the steady strength that carries you through challenges, the patience that grounds you, and the calm that radiates from your core. Allow yourself the grace to rest without judgement and the courage to accept that in stillness, resilience quietly blooms.

Affirmation: May stillness nurture your soul and restore your heart.

3rd October
The Beauty of Small Moments

Life's treasures often appear in quiet, fleeting moments — the rustle of leaves, a bird's song, or sunlight touching your skin in a gentle arc. Today, allow yourself to notice these fleeting gifts and let them lift your heart. Even in times of difficulty, life offers subtle beauty, each instance reminding you of hope, quiet joy, and the resilience that endures through every season. Observe these small marvels with gentle attention, letting them remind you that even the simplest moments can carry profound meaning.

Affirmation: May you recognise and savour the small joys that surround you.

4th October
The Courage to Trust

Trust is a quiet strength, guiding you forward even when the path feels uncertain or shadowed. Today, lean into trust — in yourself, your journey, and the unfolding of life's gentle patterns. Courage is not the absence of fear, but the willingness to move forward with hope, patience, and quiet faith. Let yourself release control over what you cannot change and allow the rhythm of life to lead you softly. In doing so, you nurture both your spirit and your heart, and cultivate a resilient trust that carries you onward.

Affirmation: May you trust in your own heart and the path that lies ahead.

5th October
The Gift of Patience

Patience is a silent companion, teaching you that healing and understanding unfold in their own time. Today, move gently through your hours, breathing fully, and honour the quiet pace of your own journey. Even in waiting, there is meaning, subtle growth, and a nurturing power that strengthens the spirit. Allow the slow rhythms of life to guide your steps, remembering that every pause, every gentle action, is a testament to the resilience within you. Patience is not idle — it is an active practice of care for yourself and your world.

Affirmation: May patience guide your heart, filling you with calm, trust, and quiet strength.

6th October
The Whisper of Hope

Hope often arrives as a gentle whisper, subtle yet insistent, reminding you that even in moments of shadow, light exists. Today, attune your heart to its delicate voice, noticing how it lifts you, guides you, and illuminates the path before you. Even when uncertainty or fatigue weighs upon your spirit, hope carries quiet courage, sustaining you and inspiring renewal. Let it flow through your mind and body, a tender companion that encourages you to move forward with gentle determination.

Affirmation: May hope whisper softly to your heart, guiding and sustaining you.

7th October
The River of Light

A river flows with gentle might,
Through shadowed valleys, into light.
Its waters shimmer, soft and clear,
Whispering courage into your ear.
Even when storms have crossed your way,
The river moves, persistent and brave.
Step softly in, feel its embrace,
Let every ripple restore your grace.
Through trials faced and nights endured,
The river carries hope assured.
Let its current guide your heart,
A quiet companion, never apart.
Trust in its rhythm, calm and true,
And let the river flow within you.

Affirmation: You are carried by the steady, gentle current of life.

8th October
The Flow of Life

Life flows like a tender stream, its gentle currents weaving through moments of joy, challenge, and reflection. A seal glides with silent grace beneath the autumnal waves, a poetic dance upon the ocean's deepening embrace as the season turns. Today, notice the ebb and flow of experience, the rhythm of your breath mirroring the tide's soft cadence, and the subtle guidance of your inner wisdom, a serene beacon reflected in the seal's tranquil drift across the misty sea. Each small movement forward is proof of your resilience and courage, a steadfast journey akin to the stream's unyielding path through the russet landscape, while each pause offers an opportunity to nourish your spirit, a quiet sanctuary amidst the distant calls of gulls riding the autumn breeze. Let yourself follow the stream with gentleness, trusting that every twist and turn is a part of your unique journey, a harmonious voyage guided by the seal's wisdom and the ocean's timeless rhythm under the October sky, where leaves fall like whispers on the shore.

Affirmation: May you move with life's gentle current, trusting in your inner guidance.

9th October
The Light in Every Moment

Even the simplest moments carry light — a smile, a warm thought, the touch of sunlight. Today, allow these sparks to illuminate your heart and remind you of the enduring beauty that surrounds you. Life is composed of countless subtle glimmers, each one an invitation to notice hope, resilience, and joy. By welcoming them, you feed your spirit and create space for gratitude and peace to flourish within you.

Affirmation: May you see and embrace the light present in every moment.

10th October
The Strength in Patience

Patience is a quiet strength, allowing healing and growth to unfold naturally. Today, move gently through your day, trusting that each moment nurtures your inner resilience. Even in waiting, you are supported, guided, and strengthened by life's subtle rhythms. Every pause, every breath, is an act of care that honours your journey, reminding you that strength often resides in stillness and gentle persistence.

Affirmation: May patience nurture your heart and strengthen your spirit.

11th October
The Courage to Feel

Allow yourself to feel fully today — joy, sorrow, hope, or fear — without judgement. Each emotion is a thread in the rich tapestry of your life, adding depth, colour, and meaning. By honouring your feelings, you create space for healing, understanding, and the gentle strengthening of your spirit. Today, each heartbeat is a sign of courage, each tear a testament to your tender resilience.

Affirmation: May you feel fully, trusting that every emotion nurtures your growth.

12th October
The Tenderness of Self-Kindness

Speak softly to your own heart today, offering yourself the compassion you naturally give to others. Recognise your resilience, your patience, and the quiet victories that often go unseen. Each act of self-kindness — a mindful breath, a small pause, a warm thought — nourishes your spirit and illuminates the inner strength that carries you. Let tenderness guide your words, actions, and thoughts, creating a sanctuary of care within yourself.

Affirmation: May you nurture yourself with tenderness, compassion, and understanding.

13th October
The Beauty of Small Joys

Life's treasures often appear in subtle, fleeting moments — a bird's song, the fragrance of flowers, or a quiet smile shared with a friend. Today, notice these small joys and allow them to uplift your heart. Even the simplest pleasures remind you that beauty persists, offering hope, comfort, and gentle inspiration. Let yourself linger in their presence, letting gratitude and delight wash softly through your spirit.

Affirmation: May you recognise and delight in the small joys that surround you.

14th October
The Garden of Light

Within your heart, a garden blooms,
Softly dispelling the darkest glooms.
Each leaf, each flower, each tender vine,
Whispers that hope will always shine.
Even when storms have crossed your sky,
Roots hold firm, reaching high.
Patience waters, love gives sun,
Guiding each bloom until it's won.
Through trials faced and quiet fears,
The garden awakens across the years.
Step gently in, feel its embrace,
Let every flower reflect your grace.
Carry its warmth within your heart,
A luminous guide as days depart.

Affirmation: You cultivate hope, patience, and light within your heart.

15th October
Amber Light

The morning unfurls in soft shades of amber, a warm and gentle glow that caresses the crisp autumn air, where a seal rests with tranquil poise upon the rugged shore, a poetic emblem of nature's enduring grace amidst the turning season's embrace. You notice the way light touches your skin, small yet significant, a tender whisper of quiet beauty that persists even amidst challenge, mirrored by the seal's serene drift beneath the misty waves and the distant cry of gulls. Your body, tender and strong like the ancient oaks shedding their leaves, asks for care, and you respond with kindness, a compassionate dance guided by the rustling winds of October's twilight. Each breath becomes a gentle acknowledgement of presence, a sacred rhythm woven into the fabric of the day, while each pause transforms into a gift, a haven of peace where the sea murmurs its wisdom under the amber sky. Today, you allow yourself to move slowly, embracing patience and self-compassion as your faithful companions, a harmonious journey reflected in the seal's unhurried grace and the ocean's timeless lullaby as autumn deepens its quiet beauty.

Affirmation: You move gently through your day, carrying patience and care.

16th October
Falling Gold

Leaves drift lazily to the ground, turning as they fall, a soft dance of amber and gold. You feel that same rhythm within yourself — surrender and strength intertwined. Even when fatigue tugs at your body or worry whispers in your mind, you can let go gently, trusting in the subtle power of presence. Today, every breath, every mindful pause, nurtures your spirit.

Affirmation: You release what no longer serves you with gentle trust.

17th October
Crimson Hues

The trees glow in muted crimson, a reminder that even endings can be beautiful. You notice the warmth in these colours and allow it to seep into your heart. Your journey, marked by both struggle and triumph, mirrors this quiet brilliance. Today, you move with tenderness, noticing the small gestures of care you give yourself, and honouring your resilience.

Affirmation: You find beauty and courage in all stages of your journey.

18th October
Misty Mornings

A thin mist curls around the garden, softening edges and blurring the world. You walk slowly through it, noticing each detail as though seeing it for the first time. Even when energy feels thin, there is grace in your gentle awareness. Today, each inhalation brings calm, each exhalation releases tension. You are present, and that presence itself is a quiet triumph.

Affirmation: You are steady and present, even in gentle stillness.

19th October
Silvered Branches

Frost glimmers lightly on the edges of the bare branches, delicate and transient. You see yourself mirrored in this quiet beauty — enduring, luminous, patient. Even in moments of uncertainty, you carry an inner light. Today, nurture this resilience with soft gestures and gentle attention. Every breath, every pause, is enough to sustain you.

Affirmation: You are resilient, delicate yet strong.

20th October
Autumn's Whisper

Leaves fall softly, one by one,
Amber and gold beneath the sun.
Branches bend with patient grace,
Whispering courage in this quiet space.
Shadows lengthen, light softens the ground,
In stillness, your strength is quietly found.
Each small step, each mindful breath,
Is a testament to endurance, to life, to depth.
Hearts remain steady as the season turns,
A gentle fire within softly burns.
You are held by the world, near and far,
Even in struggle, you shine like a star.
Rest when you must, rise when you may,
Autumn's whisper guides your way.

Affirmation: You are held gently by the rhythm of the season.

21st October
Dew-Kissed Path

The morning unveils a dew-kissed path where glistening droplets adorn fallen leaves, each jewel catching the soft autumn light as a hedgehog rustles with gentle purpose through the russet undergrowth, a poetic reflection of nature's quiet splendour in the season's embrace. You notice the sparkle, a tender mirror of your own quiet brilliance that shines amidst the crisp air, where a blackbird's melodious song weaves harmony through the misty dawn, a testament to your inner grace. Even when tired or uncertain, your spirit moves with subtle courage, a steadfast journey akin to the hedgehog's unhurried tread across the leaf-strewn earth, resilient against the turning tide of October. Today, let yourself linger in awe of these small wonders— the dew's radiant gleam, the blackbird's vigilant perch—allowing calm to flow through your body and mind, a serene river of peace that nurtures your soul beneath the autumn canopy.

Affirmation: You carry light and beauty within yourself.

22nd October
Amber Shadows

The sun lowers, casting long amber shadows across the ground. You breathe in their warmth, letting it calm your chest and ease tension. Life, like the lengthening shadows, shifts and flows — endings and beginnings interwoven. Today, each breath, each pause, is a quiet act of courage and love.

Affirmation: You move through endings and beginnings with gentle courage.

23rd October
Crimson Breeze

A gentle breeze carries the scent of fallen leaves, rustling softly through the trees. You feel its calm enter you, steadying your heart. Even when energy falters, you can match its gentle rhythm, moving with patience and awareness. Today, your presence is enough; your care for yourself is sufficient and profound.

Affirmation: You are enough, just as you are.

24th October
Golden Horizon

Evening light stretches across the horizon, soft and forgiving. You watch the glow settle, allowing it to remind you that even endings are gentle. Your body and spirit have endured, and this glow honours your quiet strength. Today, you move through time tenderly, noticing the beauty in each pause.

Affirmation: You are tender and strong, moving gently through your day.

25th October
Frosted Leaves

The first frost settles upon fallen leaves, sparkling like tiny jewels beneath the soft amber glow of an October dawn, where a hedgehog nestles with quiet resilience amid the crisp undergrowth, a poetic emblem of nature's enduring grace as autumn deepens its embrace. You observe the delicate resilience of this frost-kissed tapestry, recognising the same subtle endurance within your own spirit, mirrored by the hedgehog's steadfast presence beneath the glistening canopy, where a blackbird's mournful song weaves through the morning mist. Even when fatigued, each step becomes a tender act of courage, each breath a sacred rhythm woven into the fabric of the day, a testament to your inner strength amid the turning season. Today, let yourself rest in the gentle hush of this frosted landscape, noticing the sparkle of leaves and the blackbird's watchful perch, honouring your resilience with a serene pause that nurtures your soul under the autumn sky, where the air carries the promise of renewal.

Affirmation: You notice your own resilience in quiet ways.

26th October
Silver Light

The waning days of October bring a pale silver light that pours gently through the thinning lattice of branches, where the last of the leaves cling like tattered banners of gold and rust. The garden lies hushed beneath this glow, its air cool and damp, carrying the earthy scent of fallen leaves softening into the soil. A robin flits across the hedge, its breast a small flame against the muted sky, reminding you that even in the year's decline, brightness lingers. You draw this light inward, letting it settle in your chest, as though it were a lantern placed tenderly within, calming your restless mind and easing the weight of your body. Though fatigue may sometimes shadow your days, there is a clarity to be found in this gentle radiance, a beauty that asks nothing but your presence. Autumn teaches that in surrender there is grace, and in stillness, strength. Today, let each breath be unhurried, each step soft upon the earth, and trust in the enduring light that shines within you, steadfast as the turning seasons.

Affirmation: You carry quiet clarity and strength within you.

27th October
Twilight Amber

Evening drapes the land in amber tones, softening edges and inviting stillness. You pause to notice it, letting its warmth settle into your spirit. Your journey has been long and layered, and yet here you are — tender, present, enduring. Today, every inhalation is a reminder of your courage, every exhalation a release of what you no longer need.

Affirmation: You are present, enduring, and tenderly courageous.

28th October
Murmur of Trees

The wind whispers through the trees, soft as a lullaby. You feel it echo within you, quieting worry and fatigue. Even when the days feel heavy, your spirit continues, patient and aware. Today, let this murmur guide you, reminding you that gentle endurance carries you forward.

Affirmation: You move forward with patience and quiet strength.

29th October
Amber Path

Late October lays down its amber carpet, the path softened with fallen leaves that rustle faintly beneath your step, as though whispering secrets of the turning year. The air carries a cool sharpness, tinged with woodsmoke and the dampness of soil, while overhead a grey sky shifts like worn silk. A squirrel darts across the path, gathering its final stores, a small emblem of diligence and preparation amidst the season's quiet retreat. Each step you take becomes a mindful act, guided by the muted beauty beneath your feet, and each pause a chance to notice the steady rhythm of breath within your chest. In the stillness between movements, there lies a quiet courage — the strength found not in striving, but in simply being. Presence itself becomes a triumph, a reminder that to walk gently upon the earth is enough. Today, let your pace be unhurried, your gaze soft, and your awareness a lantern along this amber path.

Affirmation: You are grounded and brave in your presence.

30th October
Evening Haze

Evening drapes itself tenderly across the October sky, the world softened by a veil of mist that blurs the edges of trees and fields. The last light lingers like a fading ember, casting muted hues of violet and rose across the horizon, while crows wheel homeward to their roost, their silhouettes stark against the dimming glow. In this haze, time itself seems to hush, as though the earth has drawn a long, gentle breath. You feel this quiet calm settling into your bones, loosening the threads of worry, easing the weight of fatigue. Your body and spirit, which have carried you faithfully through the season's demands, are granted the balm of stillness, a place to rest and renew. Each inhalation becomes a soft act of care, and each steady heartbeat a small, unspoken celebration of endurance. Tonight, let the hush of the autumn dusk remind you that to be still is also to grow.

Affirmation: You are safe, calm, and tenderly held in stillness.

31st October – Monthly Reflection Poem
Autumn's Heart

Leaves drift down, amber and gold,
Stories of endurance quietly told.
Shadows lengthen, light softens the air,
Guiding your spirit with gentle care.
Your heart has faced storms, frost, and night,
Yet here you are, tender, luminous, bright.
Autumn's hush surrounds you near and far,
Reminding you always of who you are.
You are strength, you are soft, you are light,
A quiet flame in the amber twilight.

Affirmation: You move through life with gentle courage and enduring presence.

NOVEMBER

1st November – Monthly Opening Poem

Opening into Stillness

The wind bends trees with whispered grace,
Each leaf a memory, each branch a space.
Amber and gold drift down through the air,
Carrying stories of seasons once fair.
A robin sings low from a half-bare tree,
Its song a lantern of quiet clarity.
Your spirit sways with the fading light,
Finding its rhythm in the deepening night.
November arrives on a softened breeze,
A hush that settles through fields and trees.
It beckons you gently to slow your pace,
To rest in its calm, its tender embrace.

Affirmation: You embrace the quiet strength within yourself this autumn.

2nd November
Falling Leaves

The trees shed their garments slowly, each leaf turning and tumbling with a grace that belongs only to autumn. They spiral through the cool November air, settling gently upon the earth, a soft quilt of ochre, russet, and gold. A hush lies over the landscape, broken only by the scurry of a squirrel gathering its final stores, or the distant caw of rooks circling above the fields. In this quiet descent, you glimpse your own reflection — moments of surrender woven tenderly with threads of strength, each release making space for what is yet to come. You breathe deeply, allowing yourself to let go of what no longer serves you, just as the trees loosen their hold without regret. Resting in the present moment, you begin to feel the subtle promise held within every ending — a whisper of renewal already stirring beneath the soil. Today, in gentle observation and tender care, you will find all that is needed to nourish and steady your spirit.

Affirmation: You release what no longer serves you with grace and trust.

3rd November
Dew-Kissed Silence

The grass glistens with dew, delicate as morning jewels. You walk slowly, noticing the shimmer, letting it remind you of your own quiet beauty — a resilience often unseen but profoundly present. Even when fatigue tugs at your limbs, you find strength in stillness, and courage in simply remaining aware. Every heartbeat, every breath, is part of a subtle symphony of endurance. Today, allow yourself to linger in the hush, breathing in calm and exhaling tension.

Affirmation: You honour your own quiet resilience.

4th November
Beneath Bare Branches

The trees stand stripped and honest, their branches etched against a pale sky. You feel a kinship with their openness — the ability to endure, to be vulnerable, and yet remain upright. Your own spirit has faced storms, frost, and uncertainty, yet here you are, present and enduring. Today, you let your heart rest in the steadiness that comes from having weathered everything before, finding solace in simplicity and quiet strength.

Affirmation: You are resilient, upright, and deeply enduring.

5th November
Twilight Amber

The sun dips low, casting amber light across fading leaves. You pause to notice its warmth on your skin, a subtle reminder that even in endings there is beauty. Your journey has held shadows and illumination alike, each shaping the courage and tenderness within you. Today, you move gently, accepting the ebb and flow of energy, embracing moments of stillness as vital and sacred. Even in quiet, your presence radiates strength.

Affirmation: You find beauty and strength in every moment.

6th November
Murmur of the Wind

The November wind moves through the skeletal trees, threading its way between bare branches like a soft, invisible river. It carries with it hushed voices — whispers of patience, of quiet endurance, of the hidden growth that stirs beneath the sleeping earth. Dry leaves scuttle across the path, chasing one another like restless mice, while a solitary rook caws into the greying sky, its cry carried far on the drifting air. You pause to listen, letting the murmur of the wind settle into your chest, its rhythm steadying your own. Within its song, you recognise your own subtle strength — not loud, not clamorous, but present, enduring. Even when the days hang heavy as low clouds, there is always space for noticing the small gestures that sustain you: the warmth of a cup between your palms, the steady breath that fills your lungs, the kindness of simple rest. Today, let yourself be borne lightly on the rhythm of life, trusting that healing arrives as the wind does — in whispers, not in grand declarations.

Affirmation: You trust the gentle rhythm of life and healing.

7th November
Autumn Whispers

Leaves fall, soft as a sigh,
Amber and gold drift from the sky.
The wind hums low, the trees bend near,
Whispering courage for all who hear.
Shadows stretch, yet light remains,
Through quiet forests, through gentle rains.
Each step you take, though slow or small,
Marks your presence, your proof, your all.
Hearts endure as the season turns,
A fire inside quietly burns.
You are held by the world, by its soft grace,
Even in fatigue, you find your place.
Rest when you must, rise when you may,
Autumn's whispers guide your way.

Affirmation: You are held gently by the world around you.

8th November
Silvered Leaves

Frost glints on fallen leaves, delicate as spun glass. You bend down to notice their intricate patterns, tracing them in your mind's eye, feeling a quiet kinship with their fragility. Your own journey has been etched with trials, yet you remain tender and luminous. Today, you allow yourself to linger in awe at the small wonders that surround you, letting the hush of the morning soothe every ache, every worry, and every thought.

Affirmation: You notice the beauty in small, quiet moments.

9th November
Amber Whisper

The November world exhales a soft golden light, a hush that lingers over fields and hedgerows as though the earth itself were sighing in forgiveness. Amber leaves catch the glow and shimmer briefly before yielding to the ground, their quiet descent echoing the rhythm of release. A robin pauses on the garden gate, its small chest kindled like an ember against the pale air, a reminder of warmth even in the cooling days. You breathe this light into your body, allowing its gentle radiance to seep into your bones, steadying your heart and softening the restless edges of your mind. Even when uncertainty shadows the path ahead, or fatigue clings like mist, you remember your own deep-rooted capacity for endurance. The turning of the season teaches that strength does not always roar — sometimes it glows quietly, holding steady amidst change. Today, let each moment of self-care be honoured as a sacred act of love, a tender gift to the spirit that carries you forward.

Affirmation: You move gently through the hours, attending to your needs with patience, treating every gesture of self-care as a profound act of love.

10th November
Morning Frost

The first frost glitters on the garden path, fragile and transient. You feel a reflection of this delicacy in your own life — the moments that seem tenuous yet carry profound meaning. Even when your strength feels thin, you can find steadiness in gentle rhythms: a mindful breath, a soft gesture, a quiet thought. Today, each delicate act is enough, each pause is a balm, and each inhale a testament to your resilience.

Affirmation: You are steady, even in fragile moments.

11th November
Quiet Hearth

The chill of mid-November settles upon the land, the air sharp with the scent of woodsmoke and damp earth, urging you to draw nearer to the comfort of warmth. A blanket folded close, the steam rising from a cup, or the steady glow of a gentle flame become small sanctuaries, tender places in which to rest. Outside, sparrows huddle together in the hedgerows, their quiet bodies finding strength in closeness, reminding you that even the smallest creatures seek softness when the cold deepens. You allow yourself to be held in the same way, wrapped not only in fabric but in calm, in comfort, in the kindness of stillness. Your body, which has borne so much and carried you faithfully through shadow and light alike, is worthy of patience, worthy of care. Today, to tend to yourself is no small act but a quiet form of courage, a brave acknowledgement of all you have endured and continue to endure. In this gentleness, strength is renewed.

Affirmation: Simply tending to yourself is an act of quiet bravery, a recognition of all you have endured and continue to endure.

12th November
Golden Twilight

The day dims, painting the sky in muted golds and soft shadows. You watch the light fade, letting it remind you that endings can be gentle, even beautiful. You have moved through days of difficulty, and still you carry a quiet, enduring light within. Today, allow yourself to linger in the beauty of transition, noticing each breath, each heartbeat, as a small triumph.

Affirmation: You embrace each transition with grace and presence.

13th November
Falling Shadows

Shadows stretch across the earth, soft and long. You notice them without fear, seeing that even darkness has its quiet purpose. Within you, moments of uncertainty or fatigue may stretch and shift, yet they are always balanced by resilience, hope, and gentle courage. Today, you move through shadow and light with attention and care, knowing each step matters, however subtle it may feel.

Affirmation: You carry courage and hope even through shadowed moments.

14th November
Autumn Whispers

Leaves fall, soft as a sigh,
Amber and gold drift from the sky.
The wind hums low, the trees bend near,
Whispering courage for all who hear.
Shadows stretch, yet light remains,
Through quiet forests, through gentle rains.
Each step you take, though slow or small,
Marks your presence, your proof, your all.
Hearts endure as the season turns,
A fire inside quietly burns.
You are held by the world, by its soft grace,
Even in fatigue, you find your place.
Rest when you must, rise when you may,
Autumn's whispers guide your way.

Affirmation: You are supported by the gentle rhythm of the season.

15th November
Pale Mist

Morning lifts with a veil of pale mist, draping the fields and hedgerows in a silvery hush, as though the world itself were pausing between breaths. Trees stand like quiet sentinels, their forms softened, blurred into gentle shapes that seem to hover between presence and dream. A heron rises from the riverbank, its wings cutting slowly through the fog, reminding you that grace exists even when outlines fade. You move gently within this softened landscape, allowing your gaze to rest not on clarity but on the quiet beauty that lies in what is half-hidden. Though weariness may linger in your body, it also carries the memory of countless small triumphs, each tender act of care woven into your being like threads of quiet gold. In stillness, every breath becomes a testament to your endurance, every heartbeat a quiet drum of presence. Within this hushed November morning, resilience does not need to shout — it glows softly, unwavering as the mist that lingers and lifts.

Affirmation: You allow yourself to linger in stillness, letting every breath and heartbeat remind you of your strength and presence.

16th November
Copper Light

The low sun casts copper hues over fallen leaves, a warmth brushing against the cool of the day. You feel that warmth seep into your own spirit, reminding you that even in times of fatigue, there is light. Each gentle movement, each mindful pause, is a quiet act of courage. Today, allow the glow to settle in your chest, carrying reassurance and hope through every step you take.

Affirmation: You carry light within you, even in muted moments.

17th November
Frosted Silence

A delicate layer of frost blankets the earth, turning hedgerows and rooftops into a quiet silver world, softening every edge and hush of the morning. The grass glimmers like a scattering of tiny stars, each blade etched with frozen lace, and a blackbird hops cautiously along the path, its footprints delicate marks upon the stillness. You match this gentle rhythm, letting your thoughts slow and your body soften, moving in harmony with the frost's quiet patience. Even when energy wanes and days feel long, this crystalline calm reminds you of the quiet resilience that lives within. Every breath you take, each pause you allow, becomes a tender act of care, a subtle nourishment of both body and spirit. Today, walk lightly through the frost-lit hours, letting the hush of winter's approach cradle you, and find grace in the gentle endurance of simply being. In this stillness, strength is quiet, unhurried, and unwavering.

Affirmation: Today, you move gently through the day, resting in the grace of quiet endurance.

18th November
Crimson Leaves

Leaves cling to branches in fading reds, a final flourish before winter claims them. You notice the courage it takes to remain, to shimmer despite inevitability. Your own life reflects this quiet bravery — moments of persistence even when the path is uncertain. Today, you embrace both your fragility and your strength, allowing yourself to exist tenderly yet fully.

Affirmation: You embrace your strength even in delicate moments.

19th November
Silver Stream

A narrow stream winds through the late autumn landscape, its surface glinting silver in the soft, low light, tumbling gently over smooth stones and fallen leaves. The air carries the scent of damp earth and decaying foliage, while a kingfisher flashes briefly along the bank, a jewel of vivid motion amidst the muted tones. You feel the same quiet persistence within yourself, a steady current that flows unhurriedly through days both calm and challenging. Even when fatigue lingers like morning mist, or uncertainty clouds the horizon, your spirit navigates each bend and obstacle with quiet grace, learning from every ripple and eddy. There is no need for haste; the stream teaches that forward movement is measured not by speed, but by consistency and patience. Today, let this vision of gentle flow remind you that your own pace is enough, that your steady presence is itself a form of strength. As the water continues unceasingly over stone and root, so too does your quiet endurance carry you onward.

Affirmation: Let this vision remind you that forward movement does not need to be rushed; your pace is enough.

20th November
Murmur of Leaves

The wind rustles through the trees, a soft murmur that soothes the heart. You tune into this gentle sound, letting it echo within yourself, softening tension and worry. Even amidst challenges, there is a quiet rhythm that carries you, a heartbeat of calm and presence. Today, let yourself rest in this gentle murmur, noticing how life continues to flow around and within you.

Affirmation: You are in tune with the gentle rhythms of life.

21st November
Autumn Glow

Leaves glow amber beneath the waning sun,
Each a story of journeys quietly done.
Wind bends branches in patient sway,
Whispering courage to guide your way.
Shadows lengthen, light softens the ground,
Strength in stillness is quietly found.
Every small step, each gentle breath,
Is a testament to triumph over strife and death.
You move with care, you rest with grace,
Each moment a soft, sacred space.
The season speaks in colours and hush,
Inviting calm with every brush.
Through amber light and cooling air,
You find resilience waiting there.

Affirmation: You are resilient and steady, like the trees and leaves around you.

22nd November
Fallen Gold

Golden leaves blanket the path, a reminder that beauty exists even in endings. You walk slowly, noticing the patterns, the muted light, the quiet strength it takes to let go. Within yourself, you mirror this rhythm — releasing gently, persisting softly. Today, your presence alone carries meaning, and your care for yourself is an act of deep courage.

Affirmation: You release what no longer serves you with gentle grace.

23rd November
Morning Haze

A soft haze veils the morning, blurring boundaries and edges. You match this gentleness, letting the day unfold slowly around you. Even if energy feels thin, your spirit remains luminous and aware. Today, each slow breath, each pause to notice, nurtures your inner calm. Allow yourself the ease of this quiet rhythm, knowing it is enough.

Affirmation: You move through your day with calm and patience.

24th November
Crimson Mist

Mist curls around bare branches, softening the world in muted reds and greys. You feel a kinship with its delicate persistence, knowing that subtle endurance is a quiet kind of bravery. Even in moments of uncertainty or fatigue, your spirit holds steady. Today, let this mist remind you that strength can be gentle and still profound.

Affirmation: You are quietly brave and steady in every moment.

25th November
Twilight Amber

The evening stretches across late November skies, a soft amber light filtering through the thinning, frost-tipped leaves, painting hedgerows and fields with gentle warmth. A tawny owl glides silently between the skeletal branches, its shadow fleeting yet deliberate, reminding you of quiet vigilance amidst fading light. You pause to let this gentle glow fill your chest, letting tension slip from shoulders and mind alike, as the world softens around you. The day, much like your own journey, is woven with threads of shadow and illumination, moments of stillness and bursts of quiet radiance. Each breath you draw, each mindful pause, becomes a testament to enduring presence, a subtle celebration of the courage that rests tenderly within you. Even as dusk deepens, the amber light lingers, a reminder that warmth and grace can exist alongside shadow. Today, in the hush of this twilight, recognise the quiet victories held within every heartbeat and every gentle gesture of care.

Affirmation: Each breath and each pause is a small triumph, proof of your enduring presence and tender courage.

26th November
Silver Branches

Bare branches glisten with frost, delicate yet resilient. You see yourself mirrored in this quiet beauty — enduring, luminous, patient. Even when energy wanes, you hold the capacity to breathe, to rest, to observe. Today, nurture this enduring strength, letting yourself move gently through the day, aware of the subtle courage in every action.

Affirmation: You carry resilience and beauty within you.

27th November
Whispering Wind

The November wind threads its way through bare branches, carrying a soft, persistent murmur that ripples over frost-silvered fields and along hedgerows stripped to their winter bones. A red fox pauses in the distance, alert to the rustle of fallen leaves, before slipping silently into the amber shadows, a quiet emblem of watchfulness and resilience. You pause to listen, letting the wind's gentle sigh ripple through your thoughts, easing the weight of worry and fatigue, and drawing a calm into your chest like the first sip of warming tea. Even in moments of stillness, your spirit moves onward, navigating the subtle turns of the day with quiet grace and enduring strength. There is power in persistence that is gentle, in healing that arrives not in clamour but in soft, steady currents. Today, let the wind's whispered passage remind you that every small, patient motion carries you forward, sustaining you in its unassuming rhythm. Like leaves that drift yet settle safely, you too continue, tender yet unwavering, guided by subtle forces beyond sight.

Affirmation: You move forward gently, with quiet strength.

28th November
Amber Path

The path is strewn with amber leaves, soft underfoot, guiding each step with muted beauty. You feel grounded in this rhythm, aware of each motion, each pause, each breath. Even small gestures — standing, breathing, noticing — are acts of deep courage. Today, walk softly, honouring the gentle triumph of simply being present.

Affirmation: You are grounded, present, and deeply courageous.

29th November
Murmur of Evening

Evening drapes the land in a soft hush, a gentle quiet that settles over hedgerows and frost-tipped fields, folding the world into calm. The last light lingers amber through bare branches, while a tawny owl glides silently overhead, its wings whispering against the cooling air. You let your spirit move with this tranquil rhythm, allowing thoughts to soften like mist along a river and muscles to uncoil with tender ease. Even as weariness rests upon your shoulders, there is sanctuary in your own awareness, a quiet haven woven from patience and care. The crows call from distant trees, a steady chorus reminding you that even in stillness, life continues with grace. Today, let the gentle murmur of evening enfold you, and trust in the enduring strength that carries you through both night and day. In this calm, resilience feels tender, unwavering, and quietly radiant.

Affirmation: You are safe, calm, and supported in your rest.

30th November – Monthly Reflection Poem
Autumn's Heart

The wind has whispered through fading trees,
Leaves have fallen like slow, golden seas.
Shadows lengthen, light softens, bends,
Guiding your spirit through beginnings and ends.
Your heart has weathered storms and frost,
Endured the burdens, counted the cost.
Yet here you are, present and true,
Gathering courage in all that you do.
Autumn's hush surrounds you, near and far,
Reminding you always of who you are.
You are strength, you are tender, you are light,
A quiet flame in the lengthening night.

Affirmation: You move through life with courage, grace, and tender presence.

DECEMBER

1st December – Monthly Opening Poem

Winter's Gentle Hold

The frost gathers on the windowpane,
Each crystal a memory, each shimmer a gain.
Winter drifts softly into the land,
A quiet world held gently in its hand.
Your spirit pauses, breathing in the chill,
Yet warmth rises from a quiet, steadfast will.
Candles flicker with tender light,
Guiding your heart through the longest night.
The season invites you to rest and reflect,
To honour your journey, every step and effect.
December arrives with patience and care,
A time to nurture, to soften, to repair.
You move gently through the shortening days,
Letting hope glow in subtle, steadfast ways.

Affirmation: You embrace the warmth within yourself, even in winter's quiet.

2nd December
Frost-Laced Edges

The delicate frost etches the world in quiet patterns, shimmering in the soft light like lace spun from the air itself. You pause to trace these fragile designs with your mind, noticing how even cold and exposure can hold a strange, tender beauty. Within yourself, you feel echoes of that same interplay — moments of vulnerability alongside the glimmer of quiet courage. Your heart, having weathered so much, knows how to honour both fragility and strength. Today, you move gently, aware that the smallest gestures of care — for your body, your spirit, your mind — carry profound meaning.

Affirmation: You honour beauty and courage, even in fragile moments.

3rd December
Soft Footprints

The ground, brushed with frost, welcomes each step with a gentle crunch, leaving delicate footprints that vanish slowly into the white hush. You reflect on your own journey, every step a testament to perseverance, every pause a gift of presence. Recovery, like winter, does not hurry, yet each small, considered movement is a triumph. You allow yourself to tread softly, mindful of your own rhythm, celebrating the quiet persistence of being. Even in stillness, there is progress. Even in silence, there is strength.

Affirmation: You move at your own pace, and that is perfectly enough.

4th December
Murmur of Winter

A soft wind threads through bare branches, carrying whispers of winter's patience and quiet grace, rustling the last amber leaves that cling stubbornly to skeletal boughs. Across frost-tipped fields, a red fox pauses, ears alert to the faintest sound, embodying the alert stillness that now stirs within you. You feel the wind's murmur echo inside your chest, a gentle reminder of all you have endured and the quiet strength that has carried you through. Emotions rise and fall like the gusting breeze — sometimes brisk and bracing, sometimes barely felt, drifting softly across the landscape of your heart — and you allow them to pass without judgement. There is courage in remaining present, in noticing the subtle offerings of this quiet world: the silver sheen of frost on hedgerows, the hush of snow yet to fall, the distant call of winter birds returning to roost. Today, let the hush of winter fold around you like a well-worn cloak, bringing both peace and soft replenishment to your spirit. Even in stillness, life continues in its patient rhythm, and you are part of its enduring flow.

Affirmation: You allow your feelings to flow without judgement.

5th December
Quiet Lantern

A small flame flickers against the dimness of the day, steadfast and unwavering. You feel that same inner light within yourself — tender, enduring, a beacon in the quiet winter hours. Though your body may tire, your spirit persists, rising in gentle waves of hope. You cradle yourself with softness, acknowledging every act of care, every pause, every breath as sacred. Today, you need nothing more than your own presence, your own gentle tending. The quiet lantern inside you is enough to light your path.

Affirmation: You carry a quiet light inside you, even on the darkest days.

6th December
White Breath

Your breath emerges into the cold air, pale and fleeting, a visible whisper of life itself. You watch it dissipate, feeling the delicate rhythm of your own pulse in tandem with the world's gentle hush. Even moments that feel fragile — fatigue, doubt, lingering worry — are met with the quiet power of endurance. You trust that every inhalation brings strength, every exhalation releases what no longer serves you. Life, like your breath, flows in both visible and invisible ways, and you are part of its tender, unhurried rhythm.

Affirmation: You breathe in strength and exhale all that you no longer need.

7th December
Winter's Pulse

The icy wind threads through the silent night,
Silver frost on branches catching light.
Polar bears stride across the frozen sea,
Steadfast and patient, unshaken, free.
The snow drifts deep, yet beneath it lies
A quiet heartbeat the world cannot disguise.
So too, your spirit, tested by flame,
Moves forward still, though never the same.
Courage glimmers in the winter's gleam,
Hope rises steady, a soft, enduring beam.
Each step, each breath, a testament of care,
Each heartbeat proof that you are there.
Through the cold and storm, the shadows and fear,
A pulse persists, unwavering, clear.
Survival sings in white landscapes vast,
A rhythm of strength, both present and past.
Winter's pulse hums in your chest today,
A steady drum to guide your way.

Affirmation: Like winter's steady heartbeat, you endure with strength and grace.

8th December
Silver Stillness

Morning drapes the world in pale silver, as if the very air pauses to hold you gently. Frost clings to edges and tips like fragments of moonlight, delicate and fleeting. You feel this hush ripple through yourself, slowing your thoughts and softening your movements. Your breath deepens in harmony with the quiet dawn, a gentle rhythm reminding you of your resilience. Every pause, every tender gesture, every quiet moment of attention is a victory. Today, you simply exist in grace, wrapped in the soft silver light of being.

Affirmation: You are doing enough simply by being here.

9th December
Frost-Laced Edges

Winter's lace traces every branch, every rooftop, shimmering in muted light. You pause to imagine it painted across your own life — moments of struggle intertwined with beauty, each hardship revealing hidden strength. Even in fragility, there is courage, and even in quiet, there is presence. Today, you honour both softness and resilience within yourself, letting your breath, your heart, and your spirit move gently in harmony with the world.

Affirmation: You honour beauty and courage, even in fragile moments.

10th December
Soft Footprints

The snow hushes the earth, and your steps leave delicate impressions that fade slowly behind you. You consider your own path — each day of endurance, each quiet moment of self-care, a small imprint of courage. Recovery is not linear, yet every gentle step carries meaning. You move with awareness, trusting your own rhythm, embracing the soft victories that may not be seen by others but shine brightly within. Even stillness is a triumph, and even silence is a song.

Affirmation: You move at your own pace, and that is perfectly enough.

11th December
Murmur of Winter

A soft wind threads through bare branches, whispering the patience of the season. You feel those whispers echo inside, reminding you of all that has been endured, and all that continues to grow quietly within. Each feeling, whether heavy or light, is allowed to move through you. Today you stay present, letting the hush of the day cradle your spirit and fill the spaces that need gentleness. There is strength in quiet observation, and courage in tender presence.

Affirmation: You allow your feelings to flow without judgement.

12th December
Quiet Lantern

The faint glow of a lantern, or the memory of warmth, wraps around you like a soft cloak. Your inner light mirrors it — delicate yet persistent, a beacon in the muted world of winter. Even in weariness, that light endures. You cradle yourself with small acts of care, breathing in patience, exhaling judgement. You need nothing more than your own presence to nurture the quiet flame within. Let it guide you softly today, as it always does.

Affirmation: You carry a quiet light inside you, even on the darkest days.

13th December
White Breath

Your breath rises in white clouds, fleeting and fragile, a visible rhythm of life itself. Each inhalation brings quiet strength; each exhalation releases fatigue and tension. The winter air reminds you that life, and healing, are subtle and persistent, often moving unseen. You move gently through your day, trusting the rhythm of your own breath, the steady beat of your heart, and the quiet resilience that has brought you this far.

Affirmation: You breathe in strength and breathe out what no longer serves you.

14th December
Winter's Companions

Through silver woods where soft frost lies,
A stag moves gently 'neath pale blue skies.
Its breath a cloud, its step so slow,
Teaching you patience in paths of snow.
An owl calls out from a silent tree,
A guardian voice through uncertainty.
Fox prints trace the frozen ground,
Proof that courage still walks around.
Though cancer's shadow once drew near,
Your heart pressed on, refusing fear.
Survival glimmers in every scar,
A constellation of who you are.
The robin sings where the branches bend,
A hymn of hope that does not end.
Winter's pulse beats calm and strong,
Carrying your spirit steady and long.

Affirmation: You walk with quiet strength, steady as winter's creatures, and you honour the courage that carries you forward.

15th December
Pale Horizon

The horizon shimmers in muted greys and pearls, a quiet promise stretching before you. You sense the same in yourself — hope that is subtle, almost imperceptible, yet undeniable. Even in moments of fatigue or doubt, your spirit persists with gentle steadiness. You linger in the simplicity of presence, allowing small comforts — warmth, light, soft touch — to remind you of life's tender gifts. Today, you need nothing but your own awareness to feel the quiet bloom of resilience.

Affirmation: You are kind and gentle with yourself as you heal.

16th December
Frozen Lace

Winter's ice has etched lace across puddles and paths, delicate and transient. You imagine your own journey in similar patterns — intricate, beautiful, sometimes fragile, always strong. You allow yourself to feel each moment without rushing, to honour both endurance and softness. Every quiet breath and gentle movement is a thread in your tapestry of healing. You are alive, attentive, and tender, walking through winter with dignity and grace.

Affirmation: You are beautifully human, woven of strength and softness.

17th December
Weary and Wonderful

Your body feels heavy, your limbs reluctant, yet within you pulses a quiet wonder — the memory of every step you've taken, every challenge met, every moment survived. Even in fatigue, there is strength, subtle but unwavering. You allow yourself to rest without guilt, to honour the breadth of your journey with tenderness. There is bravery in softness, and courage in simply being present. Today, let your weariness be met with compassion, as the frost meets the earth — gently, fully, and without judgement.

Affirmation: You deserve gentleness, especially on your tired days.

18th December
Ice-Blue Sky

Above, the sky spreads in ice-blue clarity, crisp and serene, brushing your spirit with its quiet brilliance. In this sharp winter air, where breath rises in pale clouds and the robin sings from bare branches, you feel a hush of renewal. Even amidst weariness or worry, this light reminds you that calmness can dwell beside uncertainty, just as the fox treads quietly across frozen fields, sure of its path despite the cold. The season's stillness mirrors your own strength — not loud, but unwavering, carried gently in each moment. Your essence remains luminous, steady, and worthy, regardless of the frost that lingers around you. Today, you breathe deeply into the wide expanse of sky within yourself, as if inhaling the endless horizon, letting its radiance seep into your bones. You are steadfast, patient, and radiant in your own gentle way, a quiet flame against the winter's chill.

Affirmation: You are worthy, exactly as you are today.

19th December
Crystal Air

The winter air sharpens as it flows, clear and invigorating. You feel it awaken subtle strength within your chest, stirring courage and calm in equal measure. Life, like the air, moves through you with quiet persistence, filling every space, guiding each thought, each breath. You welcome it fully, knowing that even small movements — a step, a sigh, a pause — are acts of resilience. Let the clarity of the air settle within, bringing focus, peace, and gentle reassurance.

Affirmation: You welcome clarity, presence, and truth into your day.

20th December
Silvered World

Everything the winter light touches seems dipped in silver, softening the edges of the day. You feel mirrored in this gentle glow — delicate, enduring, and luminous. Every small act of care you offer yourself, every moment of rest, each attentive breath, builds your quiet resilience. Even in times that feel muted or slow, there is beauty, purpose, and warmth. Today, let the silvered world remind you that your strength is subtle yet unbroken, present in all the quiet ways you move through life.

Affirmation: You trust the unfolding of your life, even when you cannot see the road ahead.

21st December
The Song of Winter

A hush lies deep where the woodland sleeps,
Snow folds soft where the silence keeps.
Deer tread lightly, their eyes serene,
Strength moving quietly, calm and keen.
The fox slips by with a secret grace,
A flick of fire in a frozen place.
Above, an owl in the starlit air,
Keeps watch with wisdom steady and rare.
You too have walked through shadow and storm,
Yet hope within you kept beating warm.
Cancer could wound but could not take
The courage that rises each dawn you wake.
Now winter sings through branch and stream,
A steadfast hymn, a tender dream.
Its creatures remind you — endure, be still,
For hope is a flame that nothing can kill.

Affirmation: Like the winter woods, you endure with quiet grace, and hope shines within you like an untiring flame.

22nd December
Smoke and Sky

A wisp of smoke rises into the pale sky, curling like a gentle sigh. You feel that same motion within yourself — steady, upward, persistent. The midwinter air lies hushed, a grey heron lifting slowly from the riverbank, wings folding into the distance with the same quiet grace as the smoke. Even when the world feels muted or your body feels weary, your spirit lingers, a soft ember refusing to fade. The frost on the hedgerows glimmers faintly, and like it, you too hold light even in the stillest of moments. Today you tend to yourself with tenderness: a warm drink between your palms, the soft welcome of a chair, the gentle company of silence. Healing, like smoke, is subtle yet certain — it drifts, it spreads, it transforms. Trust in its presence within you, as one trusts the return of dawn, and let it guide you gently through this winter's day.

Affirmation: You are healing, even when you are still.

23rd December
Frosted Stillness

The world lies quiet under a pale frost, each branch and hedgerow dusted with silver, the air crisp and still. A small field mouse scurries along the frozen ground, leaving delicate tracks that speak of life quietly pressing forward despite the chill. You feel the same subtle rhythm within yourself, a pulse of resilience that persists even when weariness rests heavy upon your shoulders. The sky is a soft wash of muted winter light, touching the snow with gentle brilliance, reminding you that even in stillness there is clarity. Today, you move through the hours with calm attentiveness, pausing to honour your own needs — a warm cup, a quiet breath, a moment of reflection. In the hush of this frosted day, healing continues in whispers and small, steadfast movements. Let the winter's stillness cradle you, filling your spirit with quiet renewal and enduring strength.

Affirmation: You honour the stillness within, allowing calm and gentle care to restore your spirit.

24th December
Quiet Vigil

The long night draws close, deep and embracing. You sit with your own heart, keeping a gentle watch over the tender places within. Old fears or lingering worries may rise, but so does courage, subtle and enduring. You remain present to yourself, letting the hush of winter fold around your spirit. Each breath is a devotion, each pause a quiet act of bravery. Tonight, let yourself be held by the stillness, trusting that endurance and gentleness can coexist.

Affirmation: You are brave in every breath you take.

25th December
Hushed Morning

The morning arrives wrapped in silence, soft as drifting snow, each flake settling quietly on rooftops, hedgerows, and the frosted earth. A robin perches on a bare branch, its red breast a spark of life in the pale winter light, and a hare pauses in the meadow, ears alert to the hush of the day. You rise slowly, feeling the gentle weight and wonder of another day, each breath a quiet celebration of presence. Even if joy or festivity feels distant, simply being here, noticing the frost-kissed details and the soft rhythm of the world, honours your journey. Your survival, your continued presence, is a triumph in itself, as steadfast as the winter trees that endure the cold with patient grace. Today, you allow yourself gentleness, letting warmth and calm fill you in small, tender ways — a cup in your hands, the hush of snow, the whisper of wind through bare branches. The subtle beauty around you is a quiet companion, reminding you that even in stillness, life continues to shimmer.

Affirmation: You celebrate your own strength, in your own way.

26th December
Thin Winter Sun

A narrow band of winter sunlight stretches across the frost-dusted land, pale yet steadfast, gilding hedgerows and the tips of bare branches with soft warmth. A hare pauses in a snow-speckled field, nose twitching, ears alert to the hush around it, moving carefully yet with quiet determination. You feel that same steady persistence within yourself — delicate, luminous, and unwavering — carrying you gently through each hour. Even on days when your body feels fragile, your spirit endures, like the winter trees standing patient against biting winds, rooted yet flexible. Today, you tend to yourself with tenderness, allowing each gentle act — a warm cup, a pause in quiet reflection, a mindful breath — to be an offering of resilience. Every small gesture becomes a quiet celebration of your ongoing journey, a testament to the light that continues to shine, however thin it may appear. Let the soft winter sun remind you that steady warmth, even in subtle measure, is enough to guide and nurture you.

Affirmation: You treat yourself with unwavering compassion.

27th December
Frosted Breath

Your breath drifts in white threads through the chilled air, each inhalation filling you with subtle energy, each exhalation releasing what no longer serves you. You have done this many times before, carrying forward, letting go, trusting the rhythm of your own presence. Today, you move with that same gentle awareness, letting breath, body, and spirit guide you through the quiet hours. There is wisdom in each inhalation, strength in each exhalation.

Affirmation: You breathe in strength and breathe out what no longer serves you.

28th December
Winter Bones

The trees stand stripped to their bare bones, resilient against wind and cold. You see yourself mirrored in their upright, enduring form. Life has removed many layers, yet beneath lies a quiet, steadfast beauty. Today, you honour your own endurance, the subtle fortitude that carries you forward. You are strong not in absence of struggle, but because you continue — tender yet unbroken, exposed yet luminous.

Affirmation: You stand tall in your truth, with quiet power.

29th December
Storm Sky

Dark clouds sweep across the sky, carrying sudden gusts of wind. You remember how many storms you have faced — fierce, unrelenting, yet never breaking you entirely. Today, you hold the knowledge of your survival close, trusting that whatever comes, you possess the strength to meet it. Let this awareness steady your heart, even as uncertainty or challenge drifts near. You are steadfast, resilient, and quietly heroic in your persistence.

Affirmation: You have already overcome so much; you are capable of anything.

30th December
Distant Light

A thin streak of light stretches across the pale winter horizon as the day wanes, subtle yet unwavering, brushing frost-tipped fields and bare hedgerows with soft gold. A fox pauses at the edge of the wood, ears pricked, eyes reflecting the lingering glow, embodying quiet alertness and patience. You feel that same promise within yourself, a gentle assurance that healing, hope, and possibility endure, even when faint or distant. The winter sky holds calm clarity, and the hush of evening seems to echo the steady rhythm of your own heart. Today, you linger in that quiet knowing, letting it fill you with patient courage, each breath a soft affirmation of resilience. Your story continues, measured and tender, each heartbeat a line of gentle triumph, each moment a stanza of enduring grace. Let this distant light guide you through the closing hours of the year, a steady companion illuminating your path forward.

Affirmation: You stay open to tomorrow's possibilities.

31st December – Monthly Reflection Poem
Winter's Heartbeat

The year exhales in a hush of snow,
Time slows its turning, soft and low.
Branches glisten with silver light,
Stars lean close through the velvet night.
Fox prints cross the frosted lane,
Proof of life in the still domain.
An owl calls out from the shadowed air,
Its echo steady, a whispered prayer.
Your heart, too, beats in the winter's hush,
A rhythm strong through the season's crush.
It carries the memory of all you've braved,
Of nights endured and mornings saved.
Though shadows linger and darkness stays,
Hope glows faint but never decays.
Each breath you take is a vow to keep,
A promise alive in winter's deep.
The year now folds into quiet rest,
And you, too, pause — held, and blessed

Affirmation: You move forward with hope, carrying your quiet, powerful resilience.

ABOUT THE AUTHOR

Caroline, a breast cancer survivor diagnosed in 2024, discovered solace and resilience through mindfulness and self-care, nurtured by the compassionate support of her treatment team, as well as Penny Brohn UK and MacMillan Cancer Support. Her journey of recovery was profoundly shaped by her participation in Breast Cancer Now's 'Moving Forward' programme and Life After Cancer's 'Creativity for Wellbeing' course, which rekindled a fervent desire to channel her experiences into the art of writing.

A devoted mother, Caroline draws inspiration from the tranquil beauty of nature, the joys of travel, and the warmth of family. Though her active treatment drew to a close in 2024, she continues her path with preventative therapies. Writing remains her safe haven—a refined and enduring vessel for self-expression and healing—pursued with a serene and unwavering passion.

She hopes that her work may offer a little light to anyone walking through something that feels impossible.

For more information contact:

info@poetictrend.com

www.poetictrend.com

DEDICATION

To my children,
Your radiant wonder and endless curiosity ignite the spark of my imagination.

To my husband,
Your unwavering love and resolute support anchor me through every tempest and triumph.

To my siblings and mother,
My first confidantes and lifelong companions, your laughter, resilience, and shared memories are the golden threads woven into the essence of my works. You have instilled in me the virtues of perseverance, diligence, and the beauty of simplicity.

To my dear friends,
Thank you for your encouragement and belief in me.

To my treatment team and the organisations that inspired me and held me up,
Breast Cancer Now
MacMillan Cancer
Penny Brohn UK
Life After Cancer
From Me To You,
With the deepest reverence I offer you my most profound and enduring gratitude.

If this book has inspired or supported you, I'd be deeply grateful if you could share your thoughts in a review. Your words can help others on their journey find encouragement and hope when they need it most.

eBook Print Replica (UK):

https://www.amazon.co.uk/review/create-review?&asin=B0FPGMJNRD

Paperback (UK):

https://www.amazon.co.uk/review/create-review?asin=1919228519